1949

The Poet as Critic

Essays by

MURRAY KRIEGER

ELIZABETH SEWELL

RICHARD ELLMANN

RALPH FREEDMAN

DONALD HALL

RENÉ WELLEK

Evanston 1967

The Poet
as Critic

Edited by

FREDERICK P. W. McDOWELL

Northwestern University Press

MATERIAL from the following works has been quoted
with permission of the publishers: *The Complete Poems and Plays
1909–1950* of T. S. Eliot. Copyright 1952. Harcourt, Brace & World,
Inc., New York. *Collected Poems of Wallace Stevens.* Copyright 1954.
Alfred A. Knopf, Inc., New York. *Light in August* by William Faulkner.
Copyright 1950. Random House, Inc., New York. *Duino Elegies* by
Rainer Maria Rilke, translated by J. B. Leishman and Stephen Spender.
Copyright 1939. W. W. Norton & Company, Inc., New York. *Sämtliche
Werke* by Rainer Maria Rilke, ed. Ernst Zinn. Copyright 1955. In-
selverlag, Frankfurt. "A Prayer for Old Age," reprinted by permission
of The Macmillan Company of New York, the Macmillan Company of
Canada, Macmillan Co. London, and Mrs. W. B. Yeats, from *The
Variorum Edition of the Poems of W. B. Yeats,* eds. Peter Allt and
Russell K. Alspach. Copyright 1940 by Georgie Yeats.

Contents

Foreword

In the spring of 1965 the English Department of the University of Iowa established the Iowa Center for Modern Letters to coordinate the programs within the department which focus upon research and writing in the broad field of modern literature. The chief components of the Center are the Writers Workshop, the Translation Workshop, the Contemporary Literature section of the English Department, part of the Literary Criticism group, and part of the Comparative Literature group. By joining forces, these groups have already stimulated the study of modern literature and the creation of literary art at the University of Iowa. A first major enterprise of the Center was a conference on the subject of "The Poet as Critic," held from October 28 to October 30, 1965.

Professors Krieger, Sewell, Ellmann, Freedman, Hall, and Wellek discussed, through their papers and the informal question periods which followed their talks, the reciprocal relationships between the methods of creation and the methods of criticism. The intent was to go beyond a consideration of the poet as aesthetic or social critic, in a set or formal sense, and to explore the wider uses he makes of his critical faculties. To what use does he put them in the formation of his own poetry and methods of creation, in the formulation of his own aesthetic ideas, in the refining of his conception of the critic's and artist's roles, and in the interpreting of the work of other poets? The speakers were asked to touch upon this subject: How does the poet transform his own immediate experience as man and artist into his poetry or into his general ideas about his art? In so doing, the speakers demonstrated how the operations of the critical intellect become more precise during the process of creation, during the formulation of aesthetic theory or the definition of the artist's or critic's place, and during the act of judgment of the work of other writers. The speakers allude to, or sometimes treat extensively, the poet's evolution of an implicit or explicit aesthetic as he gives form to his own creations; in turn, we see how he tends to use this poetic in fashioning his own poetry. In short, the contributors reveal how the poet's representative works (in prose or verse) throw light upon him as a conscious—or unconscious—artist and critical mind.

In "*Ekphrasis* and the Still Movement of Poetry; or, *Laokoön* Revisited," Murray Krieger discusses one side of the poet as a critic: his realization that he works in a medium dependent on a temporal progression and that he must in fact transcend the temporal limitations which his art in some degree imposes. The poet, in Mr. Krieger's view, would agree with T. S. Eliot that the "still movement" of poetry comprises its essence and essential paradox. The poet knows that he must achieve a form that will contain, and not be destroyed by, the movements of its diverse parts. In opposition to Lessing, who insisted that the arts be kept separate, Mr. Krieger insists that poets can usefully consider the classic genre of *ekphrasis* in which a work of literature imitates a work of plastic art. In short, the poet should recognize that spatial as well as temporal components organize his poems, and that the plastic arts and poetry can share some significant characteristics. At its most typical, poetry fuses the opposing elements of stillness and movement, just as in graphic art the form of the urn stills the movement of the figures inscribed upon it. Writers seem to be conscious, in fact, of this double aspect of the urn, and they have tacitly acknowledged its ekphrastic element by celebrating it in their works (for example, Faulkner, Sir Thomas Browne, Pope, and Keats). Yeats's golden bird, at once empirically real in time and abstractly patterned in space as an archetype, also epitomizes the *ekphrasis*. The formally perfect poem, then, is one in which the poet, either instinctively or self-consciously, has managed to unite the divergent elements that we find in the urn or golden bird into an "organized simultaneity."

Elizabeth Sewell poses this question in "Coleridge: The Method and the Poetry": What are the similarities that may exist between a man's activity as poet and his other mental activities, and what specifically was the relationship, in Coleridge's case, between poetic creation and purposeful thought? Miss Sewell shows that the connection was close between the method which Coleridge used as a poet and "the Method" which underlay his work as thinker and philosopher. She finds one major characteristic common to both sorts of method. As a man's inner activities increase in intensity, there arises the possibility of an internal "allegorizing" as the best dramatization of this heightened state of being. The inner life, too, links with the outer life at its most significant; each may then possess "epic for its quality and myth for its method." Thus life and mind are united in "method" at its quintessential. And so Coleridge extended method from the point at which Bacon left it, "reinterpreting it now as a power of living, a self-allegorizing, self-constructing power through which all thought, which is to say, all interpretation of the universe, must be carried on." Thought, conducted in this manner, has also a prophetic or "forethoughtful" aspect as it pushes into hitherto unexplored areas of the mind and psyche; and it thereby becomes creative in the sense that the powers of life at their best are also "forethoughtful." In that Coleridge's commitment to such a conception of method was total, he may in fact have composed his *Opus Maximus* in his own life and fragmentary writings, despite the fact that his career as poet-prophet culminates in the landscape of Arctic desolation and splendor described in the first extended passage which Miss Sewell quotes.

Richard Ellmann in "The Critic as Artist as Wilde" explores yet another aspect of the relationships existing between poet and critic: What are the roles in society that the poet and the critic should assume? Wilde exalted the independence of critic and artist; both go counter to the values sanctioned by society and are anarchic, even criminal, in their tendencies. Wilde reversed Arnold and tried, by means of "creative criticism" (a concept paradoxically originating in Arnold), to see the object as it is not; and he refined Pater's concept of the critic as original creator to allow the critic greater license to express his own soul, to create aesthetically heightened discourse of his own, and to drift with his emotions and sensations. But the artist, when he is an individual rather than a critic, can act as well as drift. He can pass beyond subversive intent to the subversive act, as Wilde did in his sexual life and as certain of his heroes—Thomas Wainewright and Dorian Gray—did in life or literature.

After 1886 Wilde related his own life "as sinner" more closely to his aesthetic theories and found that art and morality were not so far apart as he had assumed in some of his earlier pronouncements. For the artist, crime does pay, Wilde thought, by allowing him to develop to the full his individuality. Wilde's essays in *Intentions* are subversive in their two main tendencies. On the one hand, Wilde regarded art as isolated from experience, as unreal and sterile, with the result that the artist can become a connoisseur of his sensations in retirement from society. On the other hand, he increasingly felt that art can influence a sensitive person, by appealing to his latent criminality, to flout the conventions of his society; and in this view of things, the artist himself is the pre-eminent criminal. And his work is nourished by his criminality, Wilde alleges. In "The Critic as Artist," the critic, says Wilde, becomes the artist's accomplice in crime, indicating to him, by virtue of the same disinterestedness that Wilde was to reject for the artist, the directions he might take in his anarchic behavior. Wilde as critic was able to chart the paths that he would pursue as rebellious man and artist. For Wilde, sin became "the perception of new and dangerous possibilities in action," self-consciousness the perception of new and dangerous possibilities in thought, and criticism the perception of new and dangerous possibilities in art. Ultimately, sin and criticism are closely related, since they both are expressions of the elements of risk and novelty in life and art respectively. In Wilde's scheme, then, the glorification of art became the glorification of the artist, and that in turn became the glorification of the artist's perverse and criminal tendencies as the critic may actively or tacitly encourage them. The artist, furthermore, becomes a representative figure; he not only suffers for his own sins, he has the courage to suffer for mankind's as well. As a writer who embodied his own views of the artist's role, Wilde became one of the earliest examples of "the artist-criminal" in the ancestry of contemporary writers like Genet, who feel the need to "authorize evil" as preliminary to their own regeneration.

Ralph Freedman, in "Wallace Stevens and Rainer Maria Rilke: Two Versions of a Poetic," discusses the work of two aesthetically sophisticated poets from different cultures. Stevens and Rilke were poets who, like Wilde, were engrossed in critical and aesthetic theory, but they were much less concerned than he was with the artist as iconoclast and rebel. Mr. Freedman's essay demonstrates, moreover, the subtlety and incisiveness that a poet's intellect may reveal as it attempts to define with precision his own views on art in general and his own craft in particular. Stevens and Rilke had in common a desire to fashion an aesthetic that would explain their work, complement it, and provide a larger context within which it might be read. As Mr. Freedman says, the poets have similarities in their philosophical outlook, for both were formed by the same *Zeitgeist;* but a chasm of tone divides their work. Grounds for a legitimate comparison of the work of the two poets do exist, however: they shared a belief that poetry exists as a form of knowledge, they revealed an interest in the relationships which may exist between the poet and painter, and they both wished to explore the ways in which the painter's techniques bear upon the writing of poetry. Both poets seem to have been mindful of the ekphrastic principle as Mr. Krieger discusses it, since both were fascinated with how a painter confers an identity in space to an object which had hitherto possessed a primary identity in time.

Stevens and Rilke are closely connected in their preoccupation with a central aesthetic problem of the modern age: the relationships existing between objects as they are to the senses and as they suggest a reality that transcends the senses, between what is given to us in perception and what lies beyond it. Both poets illustrate variations upon a symbolist aesthetic: both wish to define the interactions between object and knower, thing and mind, active perception and passive reception. As the differences in tone in their poetry would suggest, however, differences in emphasis obtrude in their aesthetic philosophies. For Stevens, the world is simultaneously "realistic" and "idealistic," physical and mental. For Rilke, the poet's psyche as it impinges upon the objects of his perception is the paramount consideration. Accordingly, Rilke concentrates on a dialectic between self and thing and reconciles these polarities of his experience in some overarching symbol, the Angel and Orpheus figures of his poetry.

Donald Hall in "The Inward Muse" describes the interactions he has observed, in writing his poetry, between the creative impulse and the critical intelligence. There is no marked separation possible, he finds, between these parts of the mind; imagining and judging are simultaneous activities, since, in the depths, critical activity occurs and since, in the refinement of style (which occurs mostly in the preconscious), a previously censored content can slip through. There is, furthermore, no balance maintained, in the poem or in the poet's composing, between unconscious and conscious impulses or states, since there is so little that is really conscious. But an oscillation does exist in the creative process between activity that seems to belong to the unconscious and activity that seems to belong to the preconscious. In sum, the critic within has a twofold nature: "he is the choice by over-determination from the depth mind," and he is also a "traditional critic" who creates standards which are forever "changing, enlarging, narrowing as the poet ages and reads and endures." The poet must learn, above all, then, to trust the voice of "the inward muse," so that a state of wise passivity can bridge the polarities of conscious mentality and the unconscious over which full control eludes him. The finished poem must manifest not only internal coherence but an objective iden-tity as well. The poem attains this unique existence, Mr. Hall believes, as if it were at the center of a series of concentric circles which continu-ally radiate out from it. First, an oscillation occurs "between breast and baby," external reality and perceiving mind, similar perhaps to the views which Mr. Freedman describes as animating Rilke. Next, the poem achieves identity as the subject of an imagined dialogue, then of a real dialogue with friends. Subsequently, it may be read to others, it may be published in a magazine, it may appear in a book, or it may be revised for further editions or collections of the writer's work. In each step the poem gains an ever sharper identity as the independent entity, which at last confronts, in definitive form, the analytic mind of reader, student, and literary critic.

René Wellek is concerned with another aspect of our subject in "The Poet as Critic, the Critic as Poet, the Poet-Critic." He discusses the poet, not as a self-critic and not as an implicit or explicit aestheti-cian, but as a practicing critic. Whereas he recognizes that the poet serves as his own critic when he creates, Mr. Wellek does not regard this activity as the most significant exercise of the critical intellect. Accordingly, Mr. Wellek rejects Eliot's view that the only important discourse is that provided by the poet-critic who considers literature primarily as it bears upon the creation of literary art. Whereas Donald Hall agrees with Eliot "that the critical activity finds its highest, truest fulfillment in a kind of union with creation in the labour of the artist," Mr. Wellek regards the poet's pronouncements as stimulating and pertinent for his own work but also as typically egocentric and narrow. The poet-critic all too often disregards criticism as an autono-mous intellectual enterprise and is remiss in "upholding ideas of correctness of interpretation, observing laws of evidence, arriving at a body of knowledge which we may call science." The verse treatises of ancient, Renaissance, and neoclassical writers on the nature of poetry and the function of the poet have, accordingly, little absolute impor-tance. Mr. Wellek finds the modern counterparts of these writers, such as Hölderlin, Rilke, Mallarmé, or Stevens, unsatisfying when they

compose "meta-poetry," philosophical works about the nature of poetry and the poet. Other recent impressionist poet-critics like Karl
Shapiro and Randall Jarrell have launched counterattacks on criticism, science, and intellect in general; and their work seems to Mr.
Wellek to be negligible. In contrast to John Stuart Mill or Wellek
himself, these critics are impatient with, and discount the importance
of, theory; and they reject a criticism based on well-defined principles.
Other modern writers who have been important as both poets and
critics have gradually abandoned a view of criticism as an independent
discipline and have gone in various tangential directions: toward
subjective impressionism (Eliot), the overstressing of "natural
beauty" and "morals" (Ransom), or religious orthodoxy (Eliot and
Tate).

Mr. Wellek concludes that the union of poet and critic is not
always good for either and that the more successful critics who were
also poets—Dante, Goethe, Coleridge—alternated their roles instead
of combining them. We still seem to want the whole man as contrasted
to the specialist, the poet and the critic as one person. We seldom find
an individual, however, who is equally distinguished in both capaci-
ties, who can "reconcile the conscious and the unconscious, the life of
the senses and the intellect." Granted this premise, Mr. Wellek has
reason to be disappointed with the modern poet-critic, especially with
his disregard for criticism as a creditable intellectual enterprise.

But modern literature would, I think, be a much less rich territory
without the essays of those writers whom Mr. Wellek most severely
analyzes for their shortcomings: Eliot, Ransom, Tate. The fact, too,
that so many modern poets have written critical essays of some distinction would support one of the main concepts developed at this conference; that the creative impulse is not so far removed from the critical
intelligence as it is sometimes assumed to be. The modern poet-critic is
a phenomenon we must reckon with, and Mr. Wellek objects less to his
existence than to his failure to accord criticism the same respect as an
independent enterprise that he accords the creation of his poetry. The
absolute importance of both disciplines has been the implicit assumption of this conference. The provocativeness and the pertinence of the
essays in this book demonstrate that the relationships between the poet
and his informed intelligence are manifold and subtle and that this
subject is a perpetually live one in our dialogues about literature.

FREDERICK P. W. McDOWELL
University of Iowa

The Poet as Critic

1

Ekphrasis and the Still Movement of Poetry; or, *Laokoön* Revisited

MURRAY KRIEGER

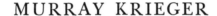

LET ME INTERPRET the proposed subject for these papers, "The Poet as Critic," as referring to the poet as critic in his poem, the poet as critic in the act of being poet; which is, in effect, to rephrase the title to read, the poetic in the poem. It would seem extravagant to suggest that the poem, in the very act of becoming successfully poetic—that is, in constituting itself poetry—implicitly constitutes its own poetic. But I would like here to entertain such an extravagant proposal.

Central to a poem's becoming successfully poetic, as I have tautologically put it, is the poem's achieving a formal and linguistic self-sufficiency. I could go on to claim, as I have elsewhere, that this formal

THIS ESSAY *will appear in a volume by the author entitled* The Play and Place of Criticism, *to be published by The Johns Hopkins Press in the spring of 1967.*

and linguistic self-sufficiency involves the poem's coming to terms with itself, its creating the sense of roundedness. That is, through all sorts of repetitions, echoes, complexes of internal relations, it converts its chronological progression into simultaneity, its temporally unrepeatable flow into eternal recurrence; through a metaphorical bending under the pressure of aesthetic tension, it converts its linear movement into circle. But, in making these claims, I am being pressed to metaphors of space to account for miracles performed in time, even if—thanks to the powers of poetic discourse—in a specially frozen sort of aesthetic time. The spatial metaphor inevitably becomes the critic's language for form. Many a self-conscious literary critic has been aware of the debt he owes to the language of the plastic arts—perhaps to sculpture most of all—in his need to find a language to account for poetry's formal movements, its plasticity, if I may use the very word that most gives the temporal game away to space.

Very likely it was just this self-conscious necessity that created the tradition of *ut pictura poesis* from Simonides to Winckelmann, the tradition that drove Lessing to the classical good sense of his *Laokoön* and its insistence on keeping distinct among the arts what belonged to Peter and what to Paul, what to space and what to time. It is surely too easy to try to make poetry and sculpture meet and even fuse (as John Dewey, for example, tried to do anew in *Art as Experience*) by seeing the poem's transcending of mere movement through circular form as being one with the statue's transcending of mere stasis through its unending movement. But still the language of space persists as our inevitable metaphor to account for the poem's special temporality, the circularizing of its linear movement.[1]

I would take as my model statement Eliot's words in "Burnt Norton" about words and their relation to "the still point of the turning world":

> Words move, music moves
> Only in time; but that which is only living
> Can only die. Words, after speech, reach

1. The beginnings of the sort of study I am undertaking here were made by Joseph Frank in his essays on "Spatial Form in Modern Literature" in *The Sewanee Review*, LIII (Spring, Summer, Autumn, 1945), which appear in revised form as the first chapter of his book, *The Widening Gyre: Crisis and Mastery in Modern Literature* (New Brunswick, 1963), pp. 3–62. But Frank is interested more in the use of these spatial metaphors by recent authors than in the generic spatiality of literary form and—even more to *my* point—in the inevitability of spatial language by the critic or by the poem as its own aesthetician. French literary critics of time-consciousness and space-consciousness, like Gaston Bachelard and Georges Poulet, also touch matters relevant to my interests here—though with a crucial difference of emphasis, as should become clear toward the end of this essay.

4

Into silence. Only by the form, the pattern,
Can words or music reach
The stillness, as a Chinese jar still
Moves perpetually in its stillness.

These words, in turn, are an echo of the words of the Fourth Tempter
in *Murder in the Cathedral,* themselves echoes of Thomas' earlier
words about the Women of Canterbury:

You know and do not know, what it is to act or suffer.
You know and do not know, that acting is suffering,
And suffering action. Neither does the actor suffer
Nor the patient act. But both are fixed
In an eternal action, an eternal patience
To which all must consent that it may be willed
And which all must suffer that they may will it,
That the pattern may subsist, that the wheel may turn and still
Be forever still.

I mean to take from Eliot's words about the still movement—like the
Chinese jar—of verbal form the suggestion that the poet himself, in
seeking to find an eloquence to account for the forms his words seek to
turn themselves into, has done well to turn to metaphors from the
spatial arts. Thus the poem that in the very act of becoming successfully poetic implicitly constitutes its own poetic may do so, as Eliot
suggests, by turning itself into the Chinese jar. It violates Lessing's
injunction most strenuously by claiming for itself another order than
its own, by substituting the Platonic claim to oneness for the Aristotelian theory of well-policed classes of Peter's and Paul's, with mutual
appropriation prohibited.

I use, then, as the most obvious sort of poetic within the poem this
anti-Lessing claim: the claim to form, to circular repetitiveness within
the discretely linear, and this by the use of an object of spatial and
plastic art to symbolize the spatiality and plasticity of literature's
temporality. Actually, of course, a classic genre was formulated that, in
effect, institutionalized this tactic: the *ekphrasis,* or the imitation in
literature of a work of plastic art. The object of imitation, as spatial
work, becomes the metaphor for the temporal work which seeks to
capture it in that temporality. The spatial work freezes the temporal
work even as the latter seeks to free it from space. *Ekphrasis* concerns
me here, then, to the extent that I see it introduced in order to use a
plastic object as a symbol of the frozen, stilled world of plastic relationships which must be superimposed upon literature's turning world to
"still" it.

There are, of course, many less explicit ways for the poem to proclaim as its poetic what I might term its ekphrastic principle, if I may broaden the ekphrastic dimension beyond its narrowest and most literal employment—as I must confess I intend eventually to do. For I would like finally to claim that the ekphrastic dimension of literature reveals itself wherever the poem takes on the "still" elements of plastic form which we normally attribute to the spatial arts. In so doing, the poem proclaims as its own poetic its formal necessity, thus making more than just loosely metaphorical the use of spatial language to describe—and thus to arrest—its movements.

A critic like Sigurd Burckhardt goes so far, in attributing plasticity to poetry, as to insist—and persuasively—that the poem must convert the transparency of its verbal medium into the physical solidity of the medium of the spatial arts:

> . . . whether [a painter] paints trees or triangles, they are corporeally there for us to respond to. . . . The painter's tree *is* an image; but if the poet writes "tree," he does not create an image. He *uses* one; the poetic "image" is one only in a metaphorical sense. Actually it is something that evokes an image, a sign pointing to a certain preestablished configuration in our visual memory. . . . The so-called poetic image achieves its effect only by denying its essence; it *is* a word, but it functions by making us aware of something other than it is. If many key terms of literary analysis —"color," "texture" and "image," for example—are in fact metaphors borrowed from the other arts, this is the reason: poetry has no material cause. Words already have what the artist first wants to give them—body.
>
> I propose that the nature and primary function of the most important poetic devices—especially rhyme, meter and metaphor—is to release words in some measure from their bondage to meaning, their purely referential role, and to give or restore to them the corporeality which a true medium needs.[2]

Thus, by calling attention to the poetic function of words as substantive entities, one might extend the ekphrastic impulse to every poet in search of the sculptor's fully plastic medium.

But, as I have said, it is most useful to begin with the literally and narrowly ekphrastic, the poems which, in imitating a plastic object in language and time, make that object in its spatial simultaneity a true emblem of itself—and of poetry's ekphrastic principle. Jean H. Hagstrum, in his pioneering work, *The Sister Arts,* finds his prime example of this mastery of space in time in Homer's description, in Book XVIII of the *Iliad,* of the shield of Achilles wrought by Hephaestus. Professor Hagstrum acknowledges Homer to be a painter, but only as a poet could be:

2. "The Poet as Fool and Priest," *ELH,* XXIII (1956), 280.

6

The passage remains faithful to the demands of verbal art and is by no means only an enumerative description. The shield becomes an emblem of the life of man: of nature and society, of the seasons of the year, and of cities at war and in peace; of agricultural scenes and the diversions of the rural day. There is obviously much that is non-pictorial: sound, motion, and sociological detail all "appear" on the surface of Hephaestus' masterpiece.[3]

In this total mastery of moving life, the capturing of it in a "still" pattern, do we not seem to have the whole of Homer's world? In this emblem all is at an instant, though it is only in time and language that its simultaneity is created. The emblem is the constitutive symbol, the part that seems to contain the dynamic whole.

From the start, as in my title, following the example of Eliot in the quotations I have cited, I have been openly dependent upon the pun on the word "still" and the fusion in it of the opposed meanings, never and always, as applied to motion.[4] Having, like Eliot, borrowed it from Keats, I have freely used it as adjective, adverb, and verb; as still movement, still moving, and more forcefully, the stilling of movement. So "still" movement as quiet, unmoving movement; "still" moving as a forever-now movement, always in process, unending; and the union of these meanings at once twin and opposed in the "stilling" of move-

3. *The Sister Arts: The Tradition of Literary Pictorialism and English Poetry from Dryden to Gray* (Chicago, 1958), p. 20. Hagstrum, trying to be etymologically faithful to the word *ekphrasis*, uses this word more narrowly than I do as I follow its other users. To be true to the sense of "speaking out," he restricts it "to that special quality of giving voice and language to the otherwise mute art object." The other descriptions of spatial works of art, those that are not made to "speak out," he merely calls "iconic," even as he admits this is a narrower use of *ekphrasis* than that of his predecessors (*The Sister Arts*, p. 18 n.). Since I confess from the start that I intend to broaden poetry's ekphrastic propensities, it would be expected that I too am using *ekphrasis* here to include what Hagstrum calls "iconic" as well as what he calls "ekphrastic."

4. There is a very different and common use of "still" in the aesthetic realm, to which I must call attention, since it is so single-minded in its rejection of Keats's secondary and more subtle meaning. The "still" of the genre called still-life painting unhappily means only "stilled," inanimate, even in a sense dead—as we are told in the equivalent French phrase, *nature morte*. This sense of the timeless, of the motionless, may recall, for example, Pope's use of "still" to deny change in *An Essay on Criticism*:

First follow Nature, and your judgment frame
By her just standard, which is *still* the same:
Unerring Nature, *still* divinely bright,
One clear, unchanged, and universal light . . .
(Part I, ll. 68–71, my italics)

How much less aware is this "still" than the pun which restores vitality—and an eternal vitality—to a word that means primarily to deny motion and sound. See Rosalie L. Colie's chapter on "Still-Life" in her volume, *Paradoxia Epidemica* (Princeton, 1966).

ment, an action that is at once the quieting of movement and the perpetuation of it, the making of it, like Eliot's wheel and Chinese jar, a movement that is still and that is still with us, that is—in his words— "forever still." Thus my rendering and free borrowing of the "still" of Keats's "still unravish'd bride of quietness" in the poem which Leo Spitzer taught us profitably to view as a most splendid example of *ekphrasis*.[5] Further, Spitzer taught us to view the ekphrastic and imitative element in the poem, not merely as its object, but as its formal cause. In keeping with the circular, "leaf-fring'd" frieze of the urn it describes, Spitzer tells us ". . . the poem is circular or 'perfectly symmetrical' . . . thereby reproducing symbolically the form of the *objet d'art* which is its model."[6] In a footnote to this passage, Spitzer generalizes on this practice:

> Since already in antiquity the poetic *ekphrasis* was often devoted to circular objects (shields, cups, etc.), it was tempting for poets to imitate verbally this constructive principle in their *ekphraseis*. Mörike's poem on an ancient lamp shows the same formal circularity motivated by the form of the model as does Keats's ode on the urn . . .

So the spatial metaphor about the "shape" of the poem is not quite metaphorical, is in a sense literal. Only a little less immediately iconic than George Herbert's poems of imitative graphic form, the poem seeks to attain the "shape" of the urn. In this iconic attempt to shape itself in the form of its content, the poem seeks to perform in a way similar to the way the urns themselves, as sepulchral receptacles, sometimes sought to perform, if we can sense them as Sir Thomas Browne momentarily does in his *Urn Burial*. For the urn, container of ashes of the dead, seems to take on the form taken by its contents in life, thus becoming a still remaining form of a form that is no more. Browne's description is magnificently far-reaching:

> While many have handles, ears, and long necks, but most imitate a circular figure, in a spherical and round composure; whether from any mystery, best duration or capacity, were but a conjecture. But the common form with necks was a proper figure, making our last bed like our first; nor much unlike the Urnes of our Nativity, while we lay in the nether part of the earth, and inward vault of our Microcosme.[7]

5. "The 'Ode on a Grecian Urn,' or Content vs. Metagrammar," in Leo Spitzer, *Essays on English and American Literature,* ed. Anna Hatcher (Princeton, N. J., 1962) , pp. 72–73.
6. *Ibid.,* p. 73.
7. *Hydriotaphia, Urne-Buriall, or a Brief Discourse of the Sepulchrall Urnes Lately Found in Norfolk,* in *The Works of Sir Thomas Browne,* ed. Geoffrey Keynes (London, 1929) , IV, 23.

8

In "the Urnes of our Nativity" we see a further circularity, a further reaching toward stillness (in both major senses): we see at once the end and the beginning, the receptacle of death simultaneously as the receptacle and womb of life, even while, as tomb, it takes on a spatial permanence in its circular imitation of the living form. This added circularity introduces new possibilities for temporal complexity in the use of the urn as the object of *ekphrasis,* a raising of it beyond the linear chronology of life's transience. These are possibilities that Cleanth Brooks seems to have foreseen in *The Well Wrought Urn,*[8] where he assembles several complex uses of "urn" in poems, some of which I shall be referring to, although, interested primarily in single interpretations, he does not press their ekphrastic implications.

There is a climactic couplet in Alexander Pope's "Eloisa to Abelard" that serves at once to summarize and to symbolize this poem's studied futility. Eloisa, now denied sexual satisfaction with her lover not only by edict and by physical separation, but even more irrevocably by the fact of his emasculation, becomes increasingly and more bitterly conscious of the tragic irony in the underlying sexual meaning of her repeated imperative to him: "Come!" She reaches the bitterness of the lines,

> Come, Abelard! for what hast thou to dread?
> The Torch of Venus burns not for the dead.
>
> (ll. 257–58)

He is the walking dead, deprived of all flame. If he defies Church and even the laws of space, his coldness yet prevents all or anything. And as his beloved, Eloisa is doubly cursed since *her* heat has not been subdued: ". . . yet Eloisa loves." And then the masterful couplet to which I want to call attention:

> Ah hopeless, lasting flames! like those that burn
> To light the dead, and warm th'unfruitful urn.
>
> (ll. 261–62)

Here urn, in its simultaneous relations to flame and death and fruit, becomes in an instant the constitutive symbol for the multiple agonies of the speaker of this monologue. As both tomb and womb, the urn is the receptacle at once of death and of love, of the remnants of the flame and of its height, of the congealing of life and the flowing of life.

---

8. *The Well Wrought Urn: Studies in the Structure of Poetry* (New York, 1947). He discusses "urn" in Donne's "The Canonization," Shakespeare's "The Phoenix and the Turtle," Gray's "Elegy Written in a Country Churchyard," and Keats's "Ode on a Grecian Urn." See pp. 16–20, 101, 112–13, 139–52.

9

And a few lines later, in as daring an image, Pope adds the needed liquid element, derived of course from her tears:

> In seas of flame my plunging soul is drown'd,
> While altars blaze, and angels tremble round.
>
> (ll. 275–76)

What is left but for her to direct her flames toward God, as Abelard's rival, in the questionable frenzy of religious ecstasy?

My point is that it is the urn of line 262 that, if I may pun myself, *receives* these meanings, at once preserves and gives life to them, as it gives life to the poem. Receiver of death as it is not permitted to be the vessel of life, it is warmed by the "hopeless, lasting flames" of a desire that dare not—indeed cannot—feed it. And the flames are at once of heat and of cold: at once agent of sexuality, of the life that is its consequence, and agent of the ashes, cold residue of life's flames and death's. The enforced, permanent chastity, this death in the midst of life, is of course reminiscent of the double-edged "stillness," the always-in-motion but never-to-be-completed action that, as with Keats's urn, accompanies the introduction, in accordance with the ekphrastic principle, of spatial forms within literature's temporality.

How different at all is Shakespeare's introduction of the urn at the close of "The Phoenix and the Turtle," to be at once the repository of the separate ashes of the ideal lovers and the guarantor of their resurrection in the "mutual flame" of their newborn union, in accordance with the Phoenix riddle? Or Donne's introduction of the "well wrought urn" in "The Canonization" as the equivalent of his poem, an ever self-renewed memorial to his true lovers? Both of these uses have been properly exploited by Cleanth Brooks in his appropriately titled book.[9] Or we may move forward in time, across the centuries to William Faulkner's *Light in August,* to see the urn crucially, and similarly, functioning. It has been pointed out [10] that each of the three major strands of the novel derives its symbolic characterization in metaphorical and ekphrastic descriptions that by now should sound familiar to us. Let me cite the three passages.

The indomitable Lena Grove, in her endless and endlessly routine —even automatic—movements is, properly enough, given an ekphrastic symbol:

9. *Ibid.,* pp. 17–20.

10. C. Hugh Holman, "The Unity of Faulkner's *Light in August,*" *PMLA,* LXXIII (1958), 155–66, especially pp. 159, 161, 164. There is reference here also to Norman H. Pearson's treatment of Lena in terms of Keats's "Grecian Urn" in his "Lena Grove," *Shenandoah,* III (1952), 3–7. Faulkner's awareness of Keats's urn as a source for allusion is more explicitly shown us in *The Bear.*

. . . backrolling now behind her a long monotonous succession of peaceful and undeviating changes from day to dark and dark to day again, through which she advanced in identical and anonymous and deliberate wagons as through a succession of creakwheeled and limpeared avatars, like something moving forever and without progress across an urn.[11]

Continual, deliberate advance, a "succession," yet a forever movement, "without progress." The rolling wheels of all the interchangeable wagons are not finally very different from the wheel spoken of by Becket and the Fourth Tempter in Eliot's *Murder in the Cathedral;* for, like that wheel, these are fixed in an eternal motion, at once action and patience, action and the suffering of action (with the appropriate puns on "patience" and "suffering"). The eternal circularity of Lena's urn and the wagon wheels that bear her round it is further enhanced by the transcendent notion of the "avatars": the god in an ever reappearing, ever indestructible, ever freshly embodied movement, continually in touch with the world and yet remaining intact.

There are similarly definitive passages for Joe Christmas and the Reverend Hightower. First, the young Joe Christmas' vision after his discovery of the uglier facts about female physiology:

In the notseeing and the hardknowing as though in a cave he seemed to see a diminishing row of suavely shaped urns in moonlight, blanched. And not one was perfect. Each one was cracked and from each crack there issued something liquid, deathcolored, and foul. He touched a tree, leaning his propped arms against it, seeing the ranked and moonlit urns. He vomited. (P. 165)

Then Hightower's vision of the "seminary," that etymologically shrewd word, as the protected retreat from living, as the tomb of the seed killed within him:

When he believed that he had heard the call it seemed to him that he could see his future, his life, intact and on all sides complete and inviolable, like a classic and serene vase, where the spirit could be born anew sheltered from the harsh gale of living and die so, peacefully, with only the far sound of the circumvented wind, with scarce even a handful of rotting dust to be disposed of. That was what the word seminary meant: quiet and safe walls within which the hampered and garmentworried spirit could learn anew serenity to contemplate without horror or alarm its own nakedness. (P. 419)

We should note, first, that while Joe Christmas' urn and Hightower's classic vase exist as metaphorical definitions of their visions, Lena is an actual figure on an urn of our narrator's envisioning.

11. *Light in August* (New York, Modern Library, 1950), p. 6. Other references are to this edition.

Christmas' vision, distorted by the ugliness of human perversity, sees the foulness of death flowing from what should be the vessel of life and love. Hightower's vision, rendered bloodless by his withdrawal from the living, sees the vacancy of purity in the aesthetic containment and non-commitment of the "classic and serene vase." (And how appropriate that what Hightower sees is a vase, devoid of contents, rather than an urn—a vase as the aesthetic equivalent of the urn, while resisting the latter's involvement with either life or death.) But Lena, the creature of the endlessly repetitive, generative fertility principle, is seen as an actual figure partaking of the still movement of the life on the urn. And how different an urn from those of Christmas' vision, one that holds death as part of the ongoing life process, one that—as Sir Thomas Browne saw it—holds the body of death as the womb holds the body of life, and in the symbol that recalls the womb. So there is Christmas' death-dealing vision; there is Hightower's vision that, in desperate retreat from that of Christmas, denies life as well; and there is Lena's, the vision of wholeness under the aegis of a primal sanctity. Lena's naïveté, of course, does not permit *her* to have this vision, as Christmas and Hightower have theirs. Instead, all existing rather than envisioning, she must live it un-selfconsciously, herself crawl round the urn's surface, and be made part of the narrator's vision—and ours.

I have already suggested that the shift from urn to vase, as we get to Hightower's life metaphor, is a significant one, confirming in this sterile symbol the shift from the pulsing, dark, and deathly existential concern of Joe Christmas and the Apollonian living grace of Lena's procreative innocence to the pulse-less aesthetic distance of Hightower's non-living purity. If we view the vase-symbol generally as the aesthetic equivalent of the urn, the resistance to the urn's involvement with death and life—whether death-as-life (Lena) or life-as-death (Christmas) —then we can move easily to Eliot's Chinese jar and think of the latter as an echo of the "frail China jar" of Pope's "The Rape of the Lock," itself an echo of the China vases Pope speaks of elsewhere in this poem.

In "The Rape of the Lock" there would surely seem to be no place for the urns, if we take seriously their ritual involvement with the actualities and consequences of flesh-and-blood existence. Better, in this supercilious celebration of the airiness of the world of play that resists flesh and blood, to replace them with vases and jars, *objets d'art* in the toyshop unreality of Belinda's art-world. We have just seen Hightower's more serious and less successful attempt to withdraw from the consequential world-winds lead to a similar conversion from the urn to its life-free aesthetic equivalent, the vase, whose cognate term, vessel, perhaps better reminds us that it is but an extention of the urn. For, as I have elsewhere argued at length,[12] Pope's poem is created out of a wistful idolatry of the disengaged and—in terms of flesh-and-blood reality—the inconsequential, pure if fragile, world of social play. Finally, I claim, the mock-heroic world of the lock, where empty symbols rather than bodies are the objects of rape and battle, becomes a metaphor for the poem itself, even as the "frail China jar," *objet d'art,* becomes the toyshop substitute for our blood-filled vessels of breathing life. The recurrent use of China as symbol of honor's empty equivalent for chastity was commented upon earlier by Cleanth Brooks.[13] This use is indicative enough of the transformation of the world of bodies to the wrought world of empty objects:

> Whether the Nymph shall break Diana's Law,
> Or some frail China Jar receive a Flaw . . .
> (Canto II, ll. 105–6)

> Or when rich China vessels, fall'n from high,
> In glitt'ring dust and painted fragments lie!
> (Canto III, ll. 159–60)

> 'Twas this, the morning omens seem'd to tell,
> Thrice from my trembling hands the Patch-box fell;
> The tott'ring China shook without a Wind . . .
> (Canto IV, ll. 161–63)

We may note that this very use of China as a generic term for ceramic objects is a metonym made in the spirit of Pope. Pope himself extends the significance of this metonymy in yet another passage in the poem, one whose brilliance sustains the others. It occurs in his description of the pouring of coffee:

> From silver spouts the grateful liquors glide,
> While China's earth receives the smoking tide . . .
> (Canto III, ll. 109–10)

Here in this wrought ceramic world we have the transformation of earth into art; indeed, in these earthen objects is the only earth that is admitted in this poem. China is, after all, the aesthetic form of China's earth, the aesthetic reduction of China for this social company. Again we are reminded of Sir Thomas Browne, this time his relating the purgative crematory fire to man's "earth":

> But all flies and sinks before fire almost in all bodies. . . . where fire taketh leave, corruption slowly enters; In bones well burnt, fire makes a

12. In "The 'Frail China Jar' and the Rude Hand of Chaos," *Centennial Review,* V (1961), 176–94.
13. *The Well Wrought Urn,* p. 87.

wall against it self . . . What the Sun compoundeth, fire analyseth, not transmuteth. That devouring agent leaves almost alwayes a morsel for the Earth, whereof all things are but a colony; and which, if time permits, the mother Element will have in their primitive mass again. (*Urne-Buriall*, pp. 30–31.)

The jars and vases and cups of Pope's airy world, vessels subject only to the smoking tides of coffee poured from silver spouts, are the real China of that world, from which all other earth has—by the transmuting ceramic fire—been purged. Browne helps to remind us of that more destructive purgation of earth in the fire of cremation. And the remnants of this cremation, we remember, have as their container that which also is fired out of earth. But the urn, as a created form, is one created—as Browne has already told us—in imitation of the living form as an echo of the womb which forms life. As a fired, earthen icon of what its contents had been—the earthly form consumed by fire—as holder of life and death, the urn transcends both. For it has attained the pure and permanent circularity of form and, in its frieze, has the forms of life eternally captured as, like Keats's figures or Lena Grove, they trace a still movement around it.

The sepulchral urn's aesthetic equivalent of breathing life, an equivalent that at once captures life's movement and perpetuates it, accounts for the suspended purity we have seen in the figures of Pope and Keats and Faulkner. To appropriate the term from "Eloisa," we might say the "unfruitful urn" in one sense leads to a fruitful urn— the fruitful poem—in another. There is an enforced chastity binding Eloisa and Abelard, not altogether unlike the aesthetically enforced chastity binding Keats's figures on the urn. We can see this enforced chastity in Eloisa's description of Abelard, which precedes her hopeless and bitter invocation to him ("Come, Abelard!") which we witnessed earlier:

> For thee the Fates, severely kind, ordain
> A cool suspense from pleasure and from pain;
> Thy life a long dead calm of fix'd repose;
> No pulse that riots, and no blood that glows.
>
> (ll. 249–52)

It is just this being "fix'd" in a "cool suspense" from the rioting pulse and glowing blood that lends the creatures of Pope's world of artifice in the "Rape" and the creatures trapped on Keats's urn their precious transcendence—and their unworldly incompleteness, their dance that denies the very notion of consequence. Belinda's "purer blush," Keats's "maidens loth," the mock love-battle at the end of the "Rape," the unanswered factual questions in Keats's "Ode," these testify to the inconsequential, unbound, free nature of the chaste aesthetic transmutation of breathing existence.

There are, then, three kinds of earth and three ways of its being fired—all finally expressive of the circular tradition that moves from earth to earth. There is, first, man's living earth—his flesh—that, fired by sexual desire, fills the earthly vessel with the flowing fruit of life, of more earth; there is, second, as timely consequence of the first, man's dying earth that, fired by the funeral rite, is reduced to the ashes which, in urn burial, fill the third kind: the earthen vessel, an artifact which, transmuted by the ceramic fire of human craft, becomes a permanent form. The latter is at once unfruitful and still-moving, the transcendence of earth in the earthen, the transcendence of flesh in the artifice of eternity; and—where it is urn too—it is also the receptacle of the remnants of that other earth, the flesh, that is conceived in fire and consumed by fire. Further, the urn may, as Browne describes it, imitate the shape of the human conceiving urn; still further, it may have the figures of life as a frieze forever running round it, either in pursuit of desire (the first kind of firing of man's earth) or in celebration of death (the second kind of the firing of earth) —the two very actions captured on Keats's urn. And, as in the case of Keats's urn, these are captured on the object that, as the third sort of the firing of earth, is in its shape the icon of the others and their container, holding them at once within it and on its circular surface. Thus it celebrates both time past (the ashes within) and time forever now (the circular pattern of scenes that is the frieze) , even as, in its shape, the container of death mimics the container of life, tomb as womb. No wonder an amazing, multiple pattern is projected by the purified metonymy of sexual meanings ceramically purged and yet insisted upon in "The Rape of the Lock," where "China's earth receives the smoking tide" pouring from the "silver spouts," well heated since "the fiery spirits blaze." Here is a ceramic masque, an earthen playing out of that most earthy action. Can we resist expanding these meanings to include those which range about the China vases and jars of this poem as they relate to frail sexual purity? Or, if we can consider also the "unfruitful urn" in the abortive firing of Eloisa's desires, can we resist seeing vase as the vessel that is related, without sexual consequences, to the urn, with the jar as the semantic generalizing of the ceramic impulse? We must marvel at the resuscitation of the urn, so unpromising an object of death, into a symbol of life in death: of art. We must marvel at the choice of the urn as the ekphrastic object par excellence to unite the stilled and the still-now of movement by concentrating within and upon itself the several sorts of earth and the several manners and consequences of their being fired.

But all, even the most aesthetically transcendent, still remain literally movements from earth to earth, from living-dying time to time both affirmed and arrested. This is reason enough to deny that one other kind of the firing of earth as a possible fourth kind: the religious firing that is to transform man's earth to pure spirit. Eloisa, her earth now fired so unfruitfully by Abelard, claims this different kind of firing by God: "But let Heav'n seize it [the soul], all at once 'tis fir'd: / Not touch'd, but rapt; not waken'd, but inspir'd!" (ll. 201–2). Nevertheless, this is a figurative firing only: it can move her toward the "flames refin'd" that "in breasts seraphic glow" (l. 320) only by denying her literal earth, her earthly status as creature. Which is why Eloisa remains so ambivalent, why in seeing God as Abelard's rival and successor (". . . for he / Alone can rival, can succeed to thee" [l. 206]), she must involve her sexuality in her religious impulse. She must confound the firing of her earth with the smothering of earthly fires which constitutes the religious metaphorical firing that she seeks. This denial of all kinds of earth and of earthly fires, sexual and aesthetic, replaces the movement from earth to earth with the Platonic movement from earth to heaven as the last movement, the permanent stilling of movement. It is destructive of the aesthetic, of the earthen, of the ekphrastic principle; is a fraudulent alternative and, for her, a false resolution. Time is merely stilled in the simple sense, the sense of "still life"; it is killed in the sense of the French translation of still life, *nature morte*. And the brilliant multiplicity of time's possibilities for running free and yet running around, repeating circularly, the brilliant revelations of the *ekphrasis*, of the urn at once fruitful and unfruitful—these are forever sacrificed. To alter Horace and defy Lessing, as with the urn, so with poetry.

Keats's urn, a pure *ekphrasis*, is an object especially created to celebrate the teasing doctrine of circularity. If this doctrine is aesthetically complete in creating, through enforced chastity, a fruitful urn of the aesthetic sort out of the unfruitful urn of the empirically human sort, in its chaste circularity it touches the empirically human only fitfully. In its freedom from what Yeats called "the fury and the mire of human veins," in its purging—at once Yeatsian and Aristotelian—of "complexities of fury," it asserts the transformation of the empirical into the archetypal ("the artifice of eternity"), in this way obeying the Hegelian injunction to move from the concrete to the concrete-universal. In the drama of poetry we recognize the creatures as creatures like us, like us most of all in their intense individuality, their here-and-now unique concreteness. But the motions they make—rituals of love and death—through aesthetic pattern and thus through the principle of echo, of repetition, become forever-now motions. This principle frees these motions from the singleness of chronology's linearity and of the empirical sort of finitude. Thus, though concrete, the characters in this sense attain universality. They are converted from the merely individual to the casuistic; their motions achieve formal finality even if they never merely finish. Theirs is the finality-without-end, if I may so adapt Kant's definition of aesthetic experience. As creatures fixed on Eliot's wheel or Keats's urn, they show us the movements we all are and have been eternally fixed upon making, though we each make them but once, in singleness, and without awareness of our fixed turning.

To the usual notion of poetry's archetypal nature that moves too quickly from the particular to the universal, indeed, that merely universalizes the particular, I would prefer this sense of the archetypal dimension of each poem as it struggles to capture the empirical in all its movement.[14] It must be at once as movement and as movement overcome, as movement joined and mastered, that the individual poem can make its movement eternal and still significant to us in our empirical singleness.

Yeats's Byzantium poems, as I have shown in my quoting from them, at once enunciate this aesthetic and create the ekphrastic symbol, the golden bird, that embodies it. The bird has been placed—indeed "hammered"—into these poems to continue with them their manufactured, artificial perfection forever. Purged, as the "images of day" with their "complexities of mire and blood" are "unpurged," the well-wrought object is both bird and golden handiwork even as, through miracle, it can be both at once, so that it is indeed "More miracle than bird or handiwork." Like the earthen urn or Pope's China, it is the product of the transmuting and purifying fires, alchemical medium of eternal creation, so different from the destructive fire that reduces the aged man's earth to ash. As "God's holy fire," it partakes—like "the gold mosaic of a wall"—of "the artifice of eternity," and can so transubstantiate the "aged man," the "dying animal," into the golden creature—both in and out of nature—of wise and eternal song.

Without this express insertion of the ekphrastic object, there are other birds that turn legendary under the pressure of their poetic contexts; indeed, there is a chain of them leading to Yeats's golden

14. I obviously mean here to propose an alternative view of poetry as archetype to that of Northrop Frye.

bird that may be seen as their appropriate embodiment. And always it is this Platonic opposition between empirical singleness and archetypal inclusiveness that stirs the movement toward the golden incarnation.

In Wordsworth's treatment of his cuckoo, the poet must make a judgment about this very duality in the bird: it is a "wandering voice" even as it remains "bird," it is "far off" even as it is "near," it brings the poet "a tale / Of visionary hours" even as his sense of reality recognizes that it is only "babbling." This duality has the experiential basis we find in many of Wordsworth's poems: the moment celebrated is a conjunction of two occasions, one far past with one present. The recurrence of experience, of identical stimulus, modified by the severe changes time has wrought in the experiencing subject, permits the simultaneous perception of motion and stasis that has been my concern. As his most acute commentators have pointed out,[15] Wordsworth has himself provided just the metaphor to express this trapping of temporal change: those moments, laden with "a renovating virtue," he terms "spots of time" (*The Prelude,* Book XII, l. 208) —precisely the union of spatiality and temporality I have been trying to demonstrate. The very word, "spot," related as it is here to time's movement, yet brings us to stasis, the arresting of time, by seeming to refer to a place, a permanently defined spatial entity. This notion accounts, in "To the Cuckoo," for the poet's capacity to transcend the limitations of literal reality in order, through a double exposure, to blur time's movements to an identical spot. Conscious, then, of his animistic delusion, he chooses to see the cuckoo as "No bird, but an invisible thing, / A voice, a mystery . . ." As in other bird poems by Romantic poets, the poet moves from the fact that he hears but cannot see the bird to the self-deceptive synecdoche that the voice *is* the bird, so that the bird becomes a disembodied voice, free of the mortality that attends a single finite bodily existence. Once he has thus transcended the bird as earthly animal, Wordsworth is able to return to his childhood with the claim that this is the very bird he then heard and could not find ("The same whom in my schoolboy days / I listened to . . . / And I can listen to thee yet . . ."). Now, listening still, he must—by the conscious choice of self-deception—wilfully create ("beget") that "golden time" which, in his boyhood, he shared instinctively. In this conscious decision to ignore the reality of the babbling bird for the visionary

15. None more incisively than Geoffrey H. Hartman. See his *Wordsworth's Poetry 1787–1814* (New Haven, Conn., 1964), especially pp. 153, 211–19, and his "Wordsworth, Inscriptions, and Romantic Nature Poetry" in *From Sensibility to Romanticism, Essays Presented to Frederick A. Pottle,* ed. Frederick W. Hilles and Harold Bloom (New York, 1965), pp. 389–413.

voice, he has created for the now "blessed Bird" the "unsubstantial, faery place" that is its "fit home." Dare we think the place to be his Byzantium and the recreated bird of the mature poet's imagination his golden bird? We could, if it were not that his awareness of the self-induced state of delusion leads him to remember its "unsubstantial" nature. The delusion is not firm enough to construct an object that would perpetuate itself, *realize* itself.

The poet in Keats's "Ode to a Nightingale" also undergoes the fanciful transformation of reality induced by the song of the bird. He is, even more than Wordsworth's poet, the captive of his trance, so that his fairyland demands the firm denial of the bird's material reality: "Thou wast not born for death, immortal bird!" He so uncritically accepts the magic of the synecdoche as to allow the identity of the sound of the voice to lead to the undoubted identity of occasion ("The voice I hear this passing night was heard / In ancient days by emperor and clown: / Perhaps the self-same song that found a path / Through the sad heart of Ruth . . . / The same that oft-times hath / Charm'd magic casements . . ."). Yet even here the reality principle naggingly remains. It reminds the poet that the suspension of chrono-logical time is, for humanity, not an attribute of an aesthetic never-never land, a Byzantium, but an attribute of death's nothingness ("Now more than ever seems it rich to die . . . / Still wouldst thou sing, and I have ears in vain— / To thy high requiem become a sod"). Further, the immortality conferred, by contrast, upon the bird is in effect withdrawn when the poet, awakening from the spell, admits his return to empirical singleness, tolled as he is back to his "sole self." He acknowledges the final failure of the delusion sponsored by the song of the bird, now wistfully referred to as "deceiving elf," the failure of his own fancy ("the fancy cannot cheat so well"). And the song is now permitted to depart with the departure of the physical bird:

> Adieu! adieu! thy plaintive anthem fades
> Past the near meadows, over the still stream,
>> Up the hill-side; and now 'tis buried deep
>> In the next valley-glades . . .

Beyond the "still stream," for the poet it is nothing less than "buried." Keats's poet, aware of man's need for time's movement as well as his need to capture it, has—more than Wordsworth's poet—overdone the extravagance of his earlier Platonic delusions. But he has not managed to find a material object that can contain the still perfection in an earthly form (or an earthen form, if we dare fancy Keats to be searching for an ekphrastic equivalent to his urn). He cannot travel to

Byzantium and convert his bird to hammered gold; so both he and the bird return to time-bound reality to proceed with the complexities of aging. Only the moment, but that moment memorialized, preserved, stilled—and distilled—in the poem, remains. In this well-wrought residue, the ekphrastic principle asserts itself even in the turning aside from an ekphrastic object.

How different are these experiments in synecdoche, with their attempts to hold the turning world as it turns, from the simple postulation by Shelley of the other-than-material nature of his skylark. He begins at once with the flat disembodiment of the "blithe spirit": "Bird thou never wert." But the liveliness of motion is denied together with its status as bird. Its existence in human time is by fiat transcended, so that the collision of movement with movement captured is evaded. All is stilled, and there is no living movement. One thinks, by contrast, of the urging of movement in the pleas to the mistress in "Corinna's Going A-Maying"; the conflict between moving and staying is the very principle of form in the poem. The poet warns against the dangers of staying movement, culminating in the penultimate line, "while time serves, and we are but decaying." Here movement can *seem* to arrest decay and *seem* to make us the master of time, rather than—in decaying stasis—its slave, as the "while" of "while time serves" assures us we shall be. This is the foretaste of that masterpoem about time, *To His Coy Mistress* ("Had we but world enough, and time"), and Marvell's invocation to action as the subduer of time, leading to the ekphrastic introduction of the physical, spatial object which is the emblem of his mastery over time even as time works its destructive power:

> Rather at once our time devour,
> Than languish in his slow-chapped power.
> Let us roll all our strength, and all
> Our sweetness, up into one ball . . .
> Thus, though we cannot make our sun
> Stand still, yet we will make him run.
>
> (ll. 39-42, 45-46)

Discussion of earthly birds turned legendary, of poems concerning birds that are at once temporal and supernal, must lead to the albatross of Coleridge's "The Rime of the Ancient Mariner." In few places in literature is the opposition between stillness and motion more central to the structure, and their relation is controlled by the bird as it turns sacramental. The poem swings between the movement sponsored by the breeze and the calm, the curse resulting from its being withdrawn. We are likely to agree with the first judgment of the mariner's shipmates: that he "had killed the bird / That made the breeze to blow." Everywhere descriptions of movement in its varied paces, and of calm as the dread alternative, direct the poem's own pace. The poem moves with and among its movements and calms. The gratuitous murder of the albatross marks the fall that is to stop all movement. And the mariner becalmed finds his appropriate emblem: the albatross is hung about his neck instead of the cross. It is this static, uncreative, decaying state that characterizes the poet of Coleridge's "Dejection: An Ode." The poet, in effect the cursed, becalmed mariner, asks for the airy impulse that "Might startle this dull pain, and make it move and live!" (l. 20). "Dejection" is a poem that laments the becalming of spirit, that claims failure, the failure of movement, as its subject. Herrick's "Corinna" showed us forcefully the implication of decay in stillness. Far more graphically in "The Ancient Mariner," total stillness is accompanied by decay, the decay that motionlessness permits to set in ("The very deep did rot," [l. 123]; "the rotting sea," "the rotting deck," [ll. 240, 242]). The mariner's becalmed life-in-death is a surrealistic paralysis, seven days and seven nights of the unblinking curse in the eyes of his struck-dead shipmates. In his suspended state he yearns for the effortless motion of "the moving moon" (l. 263), a still movement not unlike the movement we have marked in a Lena Grove. The gloss to the poem at this point furnishes a moving statement of such a natural, a routine motion as the mariner requires:

> In his loneliness and fixedness he yearneth towards the journeying Moon, and the stars that still sojourn, yet still move onward; and every where the blue sky belongs to them, and is their appointed rest, and their native country and their own natural homes, which they enter unannounced, as lords that are certainly expected and yet there is a silent joy at their arrival.

Later, after the partial penance by the mariner and the partial forgiveness bestowed upon him, the return of the beloved breeze and his eventual return are not of this sublime order; he is returned to his native country and to man, but as a wandering stranger among them. And, still doing penance, he must move in ever-recurrent circles among them, ever retelling his tale.

His tale, the poem proper, has movement even in the face of calm; further, as "Dejection" does not, it succeeds at last in conquering—in moving beyond—the state of being becalmed; nevertheless, it remains a "still," even-now movement. For it is framed by a repetitious, unendingly repetitious, ritual action, as the mariner must tell his tale again and again, wandering continually in search of a listener—still, even

21

now as I talk. Thus the archetypal nature of the singular, integral poetic action in its transcendence of the empirical. And thus our assurance of its casuistry, an assurance that permits our aesthetic pleasure in response to what in life would be unendurably painful. "The Ancient Mariner," in its emphasis on the necessity of the endless retelling of the tale, is a paradigm of this aspect in our greatest works. In its rounded completeness, in its coming to terms with itself—in short, through pattern, that which is bent on destroying its simple, linear temporality—the work guarantees its special, its other-than-empirical realm of being. Our despair at tragedy, for example, while preserved as despair, is yet transfigured to comfort in our knowledge and assurance of its still and inevitable movement, of how it has been and will always be—how it must be. Oedipus must pursue his stubborn ignorance identically to the identical catastrophe; Hamlet must make his always identical way to the absurd indiscriminacy of the final sword play; Lear must prance *his* always identical way to the wretched loveliness of the reconciliation scene that ironically lulls him and Cordelia to their deaths. And still they make their inevitable movements, even now as we talk—if I may stick at this point.

This is the final meaning of aesthetic inevitability or circularity—even as the urn demonstrates it; this is the final meaning of Aristotle's probability and necessity that bring poetry and its casuistry beyond history and the empirical world's possibility. The poem as total object has, despite its entrancing *movement,* become the fixed—or rather transfixed—object, its own urn, Yeats's golden bird that has been placed inside the poem to prove that the latter must breathe in its manufactured, artificial perfection forever. But, as the casuistic principle insists, it is always in its unique, contextual singleness that the poem so functions, not as a sign to the universal; in its finitude, its discrete discontinuity from all other poems, from poetry or from language as ideal forms, not as an opening to these.[16] *Ekphrasis,* no longer a narrow kind of poem defined by its object of imitation, broadens to become a general principle of poetics, asserted by every poem in the assertion of its integrity. Is it too much to say that essentially the same principle lies behind the employment of the poetic refrain, indeed behind the employment of meter itself? Such is largely the ground for Wordsworth's and Coleridge's justification of meter: the reduction to the sameness of repetition of that which is disparate, varied, progressive, in motion; the identity of recurrence together with the unceasing change of movement. It is the lack of such minute but

16. Again it is the alternative to Frye's archetypal universality that I am insisting upon.

systematic guarantees of recurrence that creates some of the handicaps prose fiction has in proclaiming itself a rounded object and that accounts for many of the *ad hoc* devices it invents to make itself into an aesthetic, a still moving, entity.

Every poem's problem as its own aesthetician, and every critic's problem after it, is essentially the problem of Keats with his Grecian Urn: how to make it hold still when the poem must move. And the critic's final desperation is an echo of the outburst, at once absolute and equivocal, of the last two lines of the poem. There are unanswered factual questions asked through the course of the "Ode" ("What men or gods are these? What maidens loth? . . . Who are these coming to the sacrifice? To what green altar . . . What little town. . . ?"). These have guaranteed the poet's exasperation at the inadequacy of empirical data before beauty's archetypal perfection, the inadequacy of fact before artifact. The final two lines confer universal absolution in that they absolve in absolute terms (to press the redundancy) the poet's need to ask such merely informational questions. We are reminded of Sir Thomas Browne's dismissal of a similar series of questions concerning the historical data surrounding his urns, "the proprietaries of these bones, or what bodies these ashes made up," questions further beyond man's resolution than those that ask "what Song the Syrens sang, or what name Achilles assumed when he hid himself among women." [17] The aesthetic of Keats's final lines, then, is the only culmination of still motion's transcendence of unarrested progression.

And so it is with the critic's desperate struggle to wrestle his slippery object to earth. It is the problem of defying the Lessing tradition, with its neat separateness of the mutually delimiting arts, and seeing the time-space breakthrough in the plasticity of the language of poetry. This language, in taking on Burckhardt's "corporeality," tries to become an object with as much substance as the medium of the plastic arts, the words thus establishing a plastic aesthetic for themselves, sometimes—but not necessarily—using the ekphrastic object as their emblem.

But in one sense the tradition from Edmund Burke and Lessing which sees a uniqueness in the literary medium *is* affirmed. For literature retains its essential nature as a time-art even as its words, by reaching the stillness by way of pattern, seek to appropriate sculpture's plasticity as well. There is after all, then, a sense in which literature, as a time-art, does have special time-space powers. Through pattern,

17. *Urne-Buriall*, p. 44.

23

through context, it has the unique power to celebrate time's movement as well as to arrest it, to arrest it in the very act of celebrating it. Its involvement with progression, with empirical movement, always accompanies its archetypal principle of repetition, of eternal return. The poem can uniquely order spatial stasis within its temporal dynamics because through its echoes and its texture it can produce—together with the illusion of progressive movement—the illusion of an organized simultaneity.

My earlier unfavorable claims about Eloisa's religious firing, like my few words on Shelley's "Skylark," were meant to serve as warning against the Platonic denial of the empirical, the mere stilling of movement. In resistance to the ekphrastic impulse, it cannot too often be urged that the aesthetic desire for pure and eternal form must not be allowed merely to freeze the entity-denying chronological flow of experience in its unrepeatable variety. The remarkable nature of Eliot's "Four Quartets," we must remember, is that the shaping of their musical form into the Chinese jar never deprives existence of its confused multiplicity. For, if we may shift to his other key metaphor, life at the periphery of the wheel never stops moving, even as it radiates from the extraordinary dance at the still center of that turning world. Yet "The Rape of the Lock" reminds us that there is a clear danger from the aesthetic purification of life. We see this danger anew if we return to the urn-jar motif and refer to yet another aesthetic jar, this time in Wallace Stevens' "Anecdote of the Jar":

> I placed a jar in Tennessee,
> And round it was, upon a hill.
> It made the slovenly wilderness
> Surround that hill.
>
> The wilderness rose up to it,
> And sprawled around, no longer wild.
> The jar was round upon the ground
> And tall and of a port in air.
>
> It took dominion everywhere.
> The jar was gray and bare.
> It did not give of bird or bush,
> Like nothing else in Tennessee.

The jar's roundedness, and—in its aesthetic "dominion everywhere"—its grayness and bareness, do no justice to the sprawling "slovenly wilderness" that surrounds its hilltop heights. (Indeed, it is only the jar's round presence that forces the formal impulse to attribute the function of "surrounding" to the aimless wilderness.) Only transcendent, the jar has nothing of life—"of bird or bush"—in it.[18] Here is the warning against the deadening of life, the freezing of movement, caused by too simple and Platonic a sense of aesthetic purity, of the jar or urn motif which, in my ekphrastic mood, I have described admiringly only. Time, in its unique empirical particularity, must always be celebrated in its flow even as we arrest it to make its movement a forever-now movement. Or else poetry is hardened into static, Platonic discourse that has lost touch with—indeed, that disdains to touch—our existential motions. But as poetry, even Stevens' poem, in its persistence, itself becomes the jar, though more insistently involved with flowing existence than was the hilltop jar it decries. Like Eliot's, it has absorbed a liveliness whose moving slovenliness it must cherish.

Writers on time in the vitalistic tradition of Bergson have commonly claimed that, in its inevitable universalizing, language tends to give death to the dynamism of experience by spatializing it and thus freezing its undemarcated ceaseless flow of unrepeatable and indefinable, un-entitied units. Thus phenomenological literary critics in the spirit of this tradition have tended to anti-formalism, to the neglect of the object and the accentuation of the subjective flow in the transcription of their authors' consciousness of time. However just their charges against the spatializing, and thus the killing, power of language generally, I must maintain—in the tradition of Keats in his "Urn" and Yeats in his Byzantium poems—that aesthetic jars usually avoid the inadequacy recorded by Stevens; that the specially endowed language of poetry frees as well as freezes temporality, frees it into an ever-repeated motion that has all the motion together with its repeatability, through the rounded sculpture-like inevitability that guarantees its endless repetition. For this aesthetically formalized language takes on plasticity as well as spatiality. Through its ekphrastic principle, literature as poetic context proclaims at once its use of the empirically progressive and its transcendent conversion of the empirical into the archetypal even as it remains empirical; into the circular even as it remains progressive.

In this sense poetry must be at once immediate *and* objective: neither the mediated objectivity of the normal discourse that through freezing kills, nor the unmediated subjectivity that our idolaters of time-philosophy would want to keep as the unstoppable, unrepeatable,

18. For a very persuasive reading, together with a summary of conflicting readings of the poem and of corroborative passages in Stevens' work (especially those relating the jar to the urn) , see Patricia Merivale, "Wallace Stevens' 'Jar': The Absurd Detritus of Romantic Myth," *College English,* XXVI (1965) , 527–32.

un-entitied all; neither life only frozen as archetypal nor life only flowing as endlessly empirical, but at once frozen and flowing (like the urn), at once objective and immediate, archetypal and empirical. I would share the interest of the Georges Poulets and the Maurice Blanchots; but I would give the special liberating license to our best poetry, insisting on its ekphrastic completeness that allows us to transfer the human conquest of time from the murky subjective caverns of phenomenology to the well-wrought, well-lighted place of aesthetics. For the poetic context can defy the mutually exclusive categories of time and space to become fixed in the still movement of the Chinese jar that poets have summoned to their poetry as the emblem of its aesthetic, which that poetry's very existence, its way of being and meaning, has implicitly proclaimed. The patterned and yet passing words can, as Eliot has suggested, "reach into the silence," "reach the stillness."

Coleridge:
The Method
and the Poetry

2

ELIZABETH SEWELL

*A whole Essay might be written on the Danger
of thinking without Images.*
(COLERIDGE, letter, November 1, 1800)

ONE OF THE STRANGEST THINGS in the process of getting
an education is the discovery of what people haven't told you about. I
do not just mean the hazards of pedagogical caprice, to which we are
all subject, teachers and students alike, nor the fits and starts of
memory through which one may retain, from a set of professorial
lectures on French literature, no more than a disquisition on the
potential uses of the word "marmalade" in English poetry, and advice
on how to deal with landladies. I mean the things which simply are
not brought to our attention. I remember my own sense of astonished
outrage when, years after I had finished any formal university education, I discovered Victor Hugo's great essay on Shakespeare. I had
wrestled with Hugo at college, wrestled with the plays and the poems,
doing a little better with the political verse, but feeling all the time,
"There must be more to it than this." There was. And *there* it was, in

27

this essay, a magnificent study of the nature of genius and of the powers, scientific and literary, of the imagination. Why had no one told me about it before? Now the reason could be ignorance, to which, also, we are all subject. It could be almost administrative; thus, for instance, not once when I was studying Goethe was it suggested to me that I should look at his scientific work, and that was a reflection of the absolute segregation of science from humanities practiced by that particular university. The real reason, however, for such absences, omissions, vanishments, is, I believe, much more a question of context. Works disappear like this because they do not fit in our contemporary context. It is a context of fashion (I think "fashion" is the right word, conveying at once both levity and tyranny), fashion in literature, fashion in education, and taken so deeply for granted that we are trained to pay attention only to what is fashionable and to ignore those works which, in such a context, will not resound, will not coruscate. They have their being elsewhere.

Two such passages, or works, from Coleridge, I am taking as a starting point here, two which nobody told me about and which, when I happened on them, brought once again that shock of recognition and excitement which can be a pledge of future potential. This is, I realize, a very personal approach. Others may have been familiar with these two pieces of writing from their youth up; in which case I can only say that they were lucky. But a personal approach is not a bad thing with a man as manifold and multiform as Coleridge is. You may remember the list of Coleridgean personae, so to speak, with which Professor I. A. Richards prefaces his book, *Coleridge on Imagination*. (One of the pleasures, by the way, of working on Coleridge is the opportunity to express one's indebtedness and gratitude to those who have made him, by publication and commentary, more accessible, and this is the first of such acknowledgments.) Poet, philosopher, critic, semantics man, drug addict, genius—they all enter this list. With such a being, one needs to set some shape to one's own thoughts, and the two passages we shall work with here will do this for us. They set a kind of challenge too, for they are very different; and the job will be to see if we can relate each to other by something beside the electric current of excitement which animates and links both. They set us, almost, a kind of puzzle, which I could increase by saying that each is criticism, each is poetry, and neither is criticism and neither is poetry. Thus they fall, and do not fall, under our general heading or topic, the poet as critic, or the relations between poetry and criticism. This is good, for in the relating of these two Coleridgean works each to each I want at the same time to shake a little our fashionable context of thought, both in regard to

Coleridge, and in regard to poetry and criticism in general. Better still, I want to call in Coleridge to do the shaking for us. Now, without any further mystification, to the two passages themselves.

The first is from a letter to an unknown correspondent. I came on it originally in the Nonesuch edition of selected works of Coleridge, where the date is given as 1820. This has since been amended by Professor E. L. Griggs (what a debt of gratitude is here, for the publication of all those letters, and more still to come!) who suggests November, 1819. Coleridge begins by saying that if ever he were to be stirred again to poetry in relation to his own experiences, he would venture on "a yet stranger and wilder Allegory than of yore." This is, as it were, the prose preface to what is to follow; for suddenly as we watch it and him, the prose letter turns into a poem before our eyes:

> I would *allegorize* myself, as a Rock with it's summit just raised above the surface of some Bay or Strait in the Arctic Sea,
>> While yet the stern and solitary Night
>> Brook'd no alternate Sway—
> all around me fixed and firm, methought as my own Substance, and near me lofty Masses, that might have seemed to 'hold the Moon and Stars in fee' and often in such wild play with meteoric lights, or with the quiet Shine from above which they made rebound in sparkles or dispand in off-shoots and splinters and iridescent Needle-shafts of keenest Glitter, that it was a pride and a place of Healing to lie, as in an Apostle's Shadow, within the Eclipse and deep substance-seeming Gloom of 'these dread Ambassadors from Earth to Heaven, Great Hierarchs!' and tho' obscured yet to think myself obscured by consubstantial Forms, based in the same Foundation as my own. I grieved not to serve them—yea, lovingly and with gladsomeness I abased myself in their presence: for they are my Brothers, I said, and the Mastery is their's by right of elder birth and by right of the mightier strivings of the hidden Fire that uplifted them above me. [MS breaks off thus.]

My first sober thought, after one had made whatever gesture of recognition—perhaps one should say, of abasement, using Coleridge's own word—seemed appropriate, was, "So the ice got him at last." Ice recurs, does it not, in his poems, his self-allegories if this is what they are, the sunny pleasure-dome with caves of ice or, even more, in "The Rime of the Ancient Mariner"? But there, we recall,

> The ice did split with a thunder-fit;
> The helmsman steered us through.

Now, in this late image, he is caught in it, once and for all, only just emerging above it; and if we remember Dante and his cold deeps of hell where the faces of the damned are frozen in their turn into a lake of ice, we can sense what anguish may lie behind this self-allegory. My second thought was, "How dare anyone teach us 'The Ancient Mariner' and not tell us about this letter?" Upon which I remembered that I also had taught that poem without this staggering continuation, or gloss, simply because the latter had been unknown to me; yet it was published, by Professor Griggs, as far back as 1932.

Now for the second passage, or piece of writing. This makes its appearance, as a poem sometimes does, in more than one form. It appears as the *Treatise on Method,* which Coleridge contributed to the *Encyclopaedia Metropolitana* in 1818, and then reappears, recast, in the essays on Method in *The Friend* in that same year. Miss Alice D. Snyder, who republished the former essay in 1928, and put us in her debt for that, as also for her *Coleridge on Logic and Learning* of 1929, says of the essays on Method in *The Friend* that their importance is generally acknowledged, but adds that the *Treatise on Method* is less well known. How much, I wonder, does even the first statement amount to? Only one of that series of essays finds its way, for instance, into the Nonesuch Coleridge, and *The Friend* is difficult to obtain on the secondhand market. (This is true, in my experience, of all of Coleridge's prose except *Biographia Literaria* and *Aids to Reflection.*) As for the *Treatise on Method,* to say it is less well known seems to me to approach major understatement. I came on it quite by chance in the Rylands Library in Manchester a year or two ago; and a few weeks ago when I mentioned the work to the principal of my college in Cambridge, I found her reply interesting: "Why do I not know of it?" That she is an economist and I, technically I suppose, a modern linguist, emphasizes my point, I believe, rather than detracts from it. A work that is known only to experts in the specialized field is not known. Even among these, we find Miss Kathleen Coburn (again another name for gratitude, for work already published and the *Notebooks* of Coleridge yet to come) saying, in her letter to Professor Richards which introduces the third edition (1962) of his *Coleridge on Imagination,* "I should like to put in a word here for the 'Essay on Method' in *Encyclopaedia Metropolitana* edition, or the third volume of *The Friend.* . . . The 'Essay on Method' I find a most useful and significant document" (p. xxii). This is hardly a reference to a work widely assimilated and so recognized that we can take it for granted.

To introduce it, or both variants of it, in a paper like this, however, obviously has its difficulties. All I can do at this point is to quote two passages from it, by way of sample. We shall try to come at the substance of this work later, but I hope that these two quotations may at least suggest, when attentively read as one reads a poem, an excitement not unlike that generated by our first Coleridgean passage. In this extract, from the "Essay on Method," Coleridge is talking about the word "method" itself:

> Now in Greek it literally means *a way, or path, of transit.* Hence the first idea of Method is a *progressive transition* from one step in any course to another; and where the word Method is applied with reference to many such transitions in continuity, it necessarily implies a Principle of UNITY with PROGRESSION. But that which unites, and makes many things *one* in the Mind of Man, must be an act of the Mind itself, a manifestation of intellect, and not a spontaneous and uncertain production of circumstances. This act of the Mind, then, this leading thought, this "key note" of the harmony, this "subtile, cementing, subterraneous" power, borrowing a phrase from the nomenclature of legislation, we may not inaptly call the INITIATIVE of all Method. It is manifest, that the wider the sphere of transition is, the more comprehensive and commanding must be the initiative: and if we would discover an *universal Method,* by which every step in our progress through the whole circle of Art and Science should be directed, it is absolutely necessary that we should seek it in the very interior and central essence of the Human Intellect. . . .

Already, I think, there is the sense almost of some dark and arduous exploration or journey we are to undertake here. (The typographic effects in all these passages, by the bye, are Coleridge's own; he was as great an underliner and emphasizer as Queen Victoria.) The second quotation is taken from our other source, the essays on Method in Volume III of *The Friend:*

> Lord Bacon equally with myself demands what I have ventured to call the intellectual or mental initiative, as the motive and guide of every philosophical experiment; some well-grounded purpose, some distinct impression of the probable results, some self-consistent anticipation, as the ground of the *prudens quaestio,* the forethoughtful query, which he (Bacon) affirms to be the prior half of the knowledge sought, *dimidium scientiae.* With him, therefore, as with me, an idea is an experiment proposed, an experiment is an idea realised.

In this passage too you can hear, if you will, the poet groping forward, image by image, as he tries to reach out to the prophetic powers of the mind as it thinks forward, forethoughtful in that sense, toward its own question whose terminus is at once idea, experiment, and discovery. The Olympian phrase, also, of "Lord Bacon equally with myself," echoed a sentence or two later, is startling. This claim will have to be tested.

So, now, what do we have? We have two apparently widely different passages from Coleridge's writings, the one an imaginary polar landscape, the other a statement about Method, that is to say, mind and its ways of working. And these two we have to relate. I called this, a little while ago, the puzzle, but I am in fact cheating here, because I am convinced that the pair *are* related. They are not two totally disparate things put together, which would make them into a Nonsense coupling; something like the-argument-that-proved-he-was-the-Pope, and the-bar-of-mottled-soap, in the Mad Gardener's Song. That world of ice and the groping exploration of the human intellect are a poetic and not a Nonsense couple, and it remains now to uncover, if possible, the relations sensed as already existing between them. But this will have to be done by getting both of them out of our present context of fashion in literary criticism. We will try to do this with Coleridge himself, first, and go on to poetry and criticism, and then to *his* poetry and criticism afterwards.

What is our context for Coleridge? This is easy to answer. We know him as poet and critic, with perhaps nowadays slightly more emphasis on the latter role than the former, since he has been firmly installed by our literary educators in the stock genealogy of the great English poet-critics with which we are all familiar, running from Ben Jonson to T. S. Eliot. In my experience, if you ask people about Coleridge as poet, they will come up with "The Ancient Mariner" and "Kubla Khan" and "Christabel" and may go on to the conversation pieces, and that will be it. I just want to remind us here of all the rest —the "bad" poems, of which there are a considerable number, and one or two of which we shall be needing ourselves in a moment. What do we do with all of these? The answer is, ignore them. I often think we are much too cavalier with bad poems, those of others or those we write ourselves. They also have their uses and productiveness in the scheme of things. At least, Coleridge provides us with a good deal of material here too.

Take Coleridge as a critic next, and see what people know about him and his work under this heading. I have in mind a conference I attended a few months ago, peopled by philosophers, scientists, psychologists, and one other literary type besides myself, into whose deliberations at one point I dropped the name "Coleridge" and was much interested to observe what followed. You will get *Biographia Literaria* straight away, and within that, principally the distinction between Imagination and Fancy, plus, usually, some knowledge of Coleridge's judicious assessment of Wordsworth's poetry, and perhaps the discussion of poetic diction. You will already be doing well if you get beyond this, even if it be only to a series of phrases which seem to cling to the outer ranges of people's memories—the willing suspension of disbelief;

poetry having as its object pleasure, not truth; bringing the whole soul of man into activity; at its best when only imperfectly understood (which now, Miss Coburn tells us from the *Notebooks*, must be taken as meaning the opposite of what it has been taken to mean till now). Press further and you will find yourself back to *Biographia Literaria* again. Yet is this really all?—as one may fairly ask oneself when reading that frankly boring work for the first or the umpteenth time. All the rest of the prose, which is considerable, is ignored once again, either left unread or simply not attended to.

We shall never get our two passages together, in their proper significance, if we leave things like this. Nor shall we ever understand Coleridge, who gives us no encouragement whatsoever for erecting such a thin and limiting scheme and then thrusting him into it. Instead, let us start over again and see what Coleridge himself says that is exciting (that is to say, prophetic, having a further potential of interpretation and thought) about poetry and criticism and his relationship to each.

On poetry we will take three quotations, two from the Notebooks of 1804, the third from Marginalia of 1819:

> Poetry in its Grundkraft no less than the Vervollkommung's-gabe [*Vervollkommnungsgabe*] of man / the seraphic instinct.

> They [poets] are the Bridlers by Delight, the Purifiers, they that combine with *reason* and order, the true Protoplasts, Gods of Love who tame the Chaos.

> . . . as poetry is the *identity* of all other knowledge, so a poet cannot be a *great* poet but as being likewise and inclusively an historian and nat-

> uralist in the light as well as the life of philosophy. All other men's worlds (Κόσμοι) are *his* chaos.[1]

You may notice that two of these, the first and third, have little prose introductions, as the polar landscape did, before they plunge into poetry; and when they do, it is toward epic poetry that they plunge. The images in all three are cosmic, taking us out into those great reaches of the universe where epic poets have to venture as their peculiar task, making and (as Coleridge suggests) unmaking it all in order to renew the sum of things once more. Coleridge himself, we recall, had a sense that this was his own vocation. A vision of an epic poem he was to write swam before his eyes for many years, taking

---

1. The first two quotations are from *The Notebooks of S. T. Coleridge*, ed. Kathleen Coburn (London, 1962), II, Entries 2314 and 2355. The third is from *Coleridge's Miscellaneous Criticism*, ed. T. M. Raysor (London, 1936), Note on Barry Cornwall, p. 343.

different shapes, but never, through all the sickness and discouragement of his middle and later life, entirely vanishing.

As regards criticism, Coleridge's vision of this, and of his commitment to it, is more complex. One thing is clear: we cannot contract our view of it inside the literary pieces, the scattered criticism on greater and lesser figures in English literature, or the limits and muddle of *Biographia Literaria* ("my *poetical* criticism" Coleridge calls the latter [his emphasis], writing to R. H. Brabant, July 29, 1815). In any case the *Biographia* was originally intended as no more than a preface to his collected poems, and even after it had taken on an independent life of its own, it still remained a "Pioneer to the great Work" on which, Coleridge says, "I have set my heart and hope to ground my ultimate reputation." [2] So we come to the *Opus Maximum,* that center of his whole vocation as he saw it, which not just the *Biographia* but all his work, including some of his poetry, led up to: "my GREAT WORK . . . to which all my other writings (unless I except my Poems, and these I can exclude in part only) are introductory and preparative," as he says in a letter to Thomas Allsop, January, 1821. He refers to this "Great Work" in his books, his essays, and his letters, over and over again. Miss Snyder lists twenty-one references to it which occur between 1799 and 1834,[3] and she points out, too, the variety of forms and names under which it appears, starting as something akin to literary criticism, then merging into epic or philosophical poem, plans for education, revolution in metaphysics, system of dynamic or constructive philosophy, treatise on the *Logos* divine and human; and there are still others. Somewhere hereabouts we have to look for hints of what the word "criticism," if it is to be adequate to Coleridge, must be taken to mean.

Of course we are at once in difficulties, for the *Opus Maximum,* in whatever form, was never written—or was it? Even that is not clear. If we choose to regard it as philosophy, we find René Wellek saying, in *Immanuel Kant in England,* that the trouble with Coleridge's philosophy is not that it is nonexistent, or only fragmentary (as he points out, there are fragmentary philosophies among the very greatest, witness those of Pascal and Leibniz) ; the trouble is that it does exist and that it is inadequate. Plain speaking of this sort is very helpful, and I think anyone who has had to work through Coleridge's *Philosophical Lectures,* despite the occasional authentic flashes in them, would agree.

2. See *Collected Letters of Samuel Taylor Coleridge,* ed. Earl Leslie Griggs (Oxford, 1959) , IV, 578–86.

3. *Coleridge on Logic and Learning,* ed. Alice D. Snyder (New Haven, Conn., 1929) , p. 8.

They are dull. If, taking a different line, we regard the "Great Work" as more akin to logic and epistemology, we find Miss Snyder claiming that here, too, much more work was actually completed than Coleridge is generally given credit for. It also, in the reading, is for the most part very dull. There is something in Miss Snyder's own approach to *Coleridge on Logic and Learning,* however, which is not dull at all; indeed, it is very exciting, both in itself and in the use she makes of it. As a key motif throughout her book she uses a Coleridgean image taken from work of his which she is here publishing for the first time. It is an extended metaphor, or perhaps one should say self-allegory, of Coleridge and his reader or pupil, whom Coleridge addresses as "my Friend," making a journey together. The poet speaks of their having at length come "not only to the extreme verge of the *Terra Firma,* but to the utmost part of a narrow Tongue of Land that runs far out into the deep water." Here, Coleridge goes on, there is neither boat nor raft, but on the horizon a great ship can just be descried. He confronts us now with a decision, the more necessary because where we are "is no safe landing-place to loiter on." We may say good-bye here and go back, or take the risk of "sharing in the adventure" and decide to make the voyage "in search of the other World that *now is*": a place, he says, partly charted, partly dreamed of, and only awaiting redis-covery. The "Great Work," in its turn, may best be thought of, perhaps can only make itself manifest, under an image—once again, we notice, an image of epic. Coleridge's poems and our own chosen passage, that last terrible polar terminus he there describes, come inevitably to mind. But the juxtaposition of addresses to "my Friend," and the curious use of "landing-place" in this self-allegory, remind one of other things too; for *The Friend* has interspersed within it certain sections of lighter and easier approach, as their author thought, which he calls "First Landing-Place," "Second Landing-Place," and so on. This work of his also, as it seems, is part of the voyage we make in his company.

We are still somewhat adrift, we realize however, in regard to the *Opus Maximum:* its nature and whether and how it is related to criticism as that term may be reinterpreted and then applied to Cole-ridge. Here, once again, Coleridge is our best giver of directions, If he chooses to regard much of his work as merely prefatory to some different, main effort, there is one work, or aspect of his work, which he himself sets out in front, giving it a definite authority over the rest. This turns out to be the second of our selected passages, the other pole of our thinking and voyaging here—the "Essay on Method" and the corresponding essays in the third volume of *The Friend.* Of the first he says in a letter to H. F. Cary, January 30, 1818, "that which I valued more than *all* my other prose writings"; and in late November of the same year he tells his son Derwent that the three essays on morals and religion and the eight on Method in *The Friend,* "in point of *value* . . . outweigh all my other works, verse or prose." In selecting this work for special attention, we are, if a little outside our normal approach to criticism or to Coleridge, well within the scope of Coleridge's own expressed purposes.

What do we now have before us? Our two passages, the Arctic landscape which is self-allegory, and the works on Method; also the result of trying to reassess poetry and criticism in more closely Coleridgean terms, ending in a curious confluence of both in epic imagery. We have also one or two quite straightforward questions to answer: What is the method of the poetry? How does that method connect with the Method set out in the essays on it? Or, simply, What *is* Method?

But now already with these questions we have what we needed, a new context for Coleridge. He belongs in the small company of the very greatest of the methodologist-poets, those who were poets and who worked, as poets, on the methodology of the mind. He gives his own genealogy in *The Friend.* It goes straight back to Bacon, and then beyond him Plato, those two who, Coleridge seeks to demonstrate in these essays, worked on the same principles. Also in the family is Vico, whom Coleridge got to know later and whom he at once signed up in the company, as it were, connecting him with Bacon in a project to issue the *Scienza Nuova* and the *Novum Organum* in a joint parallel edition. It is pleasant to find "Samuele Taylor Coleridge" set down as "Vichiano ardente" in the bibliography of the big 1953 one-volume Italian edition of Vico's works, and perhaps we should remind ourselves that Vico is also acclaimed, by his editors and commentators, as a poet; indeed, I was once delighted to find him described as, in Italian literature, a poet second only to Dante. That Bacon was a poet we can let Shelley testify for us. That Plato was, needs no testimony at all. To this genealogy of poet-methodologists, Coleridge on his own account adds Shakespeare, who, for him, best represents the Method inherent in poetry just as much as in science, say, or philosophy, "by means of his intimate acquaintance with the great laws of Thought which form and regulate Method" ("Essay on Method," Section II, Head 20).

So far things have been reasonably manageable: we have a new context for Coleridge, a set of questions to tackle, and two works of Coleridge to focus on. Now, however, we have to launch out, not in command of our subject but groping rather darkly toward it through a Coleridgean universe, on a voyage not unlike the one the poet has already presented to our imaginations, where we must steer by what sea-marks and stars we can.

We will start with that poem in the letter, the landscape of rock and ice in the polar night, which will give us something definite to look at. It had, you remember, what I called a little prose preface. In this, Coleridge says that he would allegorize himself in a yet stranger and wilder Allegory than of yore—implying plainly that he has allegorized himself previously, and wildly, in his poetry. "The Ancient Mariner" rises imperiously before us, does he not, at this point? And with him can come a cluster of remarks and images on what is going on here. "Mind, shipwrecked by storms of doubt, now masterless, rudderless, shattered,—pulling in the dead swell of a dark and windless sea": that is Coleridge, of himself, in the Notebook for 1801. Miss Coburn comments that in 1796 he thought of himself as "again afloat on the wide sea unpiloted and unprovisioned," and links this with the tale of the "Bounty" and Captain Bligh, adding, "But then, was he not at moments both the mariner and the albatross?" To which one could add Coleridge saying, as again quoted by Miss Coburn, "It is an enormous blunder to represent the Ancient Mariner as an old man on board ship. He was in my mind the everlasting wandering Jew." [4] And when it comes to being the albatross, one recalls that poignant passage in his verse letter to Sara Hutchinson, the long original version of "Dejection: An Ode," where he almost wishes his beloved little children had never been born, "feeling how they bind / And pluck out the Wing-feathers of my Mind." He is also at times the sea, a sea alive and foaming with its own stars as at the end of the poem "To William Wordsworth" or that more terrible and compelling "lifeless ocean" in "Kubla Khan" where this same allegorizing process is at work.

What is going on here? Is Coleridge doing what he says of Milton—that he *is* all the characters he writes about, then adding (this in *Table Talk*) [5] "The egotism of such a man is a revelation of spirit"? Is he fulfilling his own precepts and purposes, expressed in the *Notebooks*,[6] where he says, Wordsworth's achievements so obviously and painfully before him, "O surely I might make a noble Poem of all my Youth, nay *of all my Life*"? And again there is the memo to himself of 1804, a year later than the above, "For my own Life—written as an inspired Prophet,—throughout," for which he proposes the marvellous opening: "Saw in early youth as in a Dream the Birth of the Plan-

4. See *Notebooks* (London, 1957), I, Note to Entry 45; Note to Entry 174 (22); Entry 932 and the Note to it.
5. Quoted in *Inquiring Spirit*, ed. Kathleen Coburn (London, 1951), p. 165.
6. *Notebooks*, I, Entry 1610; II, Entry 2151.

37

ets. . . ." There is a rational explanation of that, as we can see if we turn to one of his autobiographical letters to Thomas Poole, October 16, 1797; but what a wonderful way to begin! And finally this autobiography to be done in prophetic images culminates in the landscape of Arctic desolation, and splendor, we have before us. John Livingston Lowes has traced many of the images to their sources; but admirable as his work is, it is in a way almost distracting. It is the road forward that matters, the nature, uses, and prophetic power of the process here going on. For it is, if we are at all on the right tack, also the process of thinking itself and of Method in the mind; and it is this which Coleridge was concerned to explore and display, whether in prose exposition or, as here in the polar night, by vision and embodiment.

As we turn to the poem, there is no need to labor the beauty or range of it: the rock just above the sea's surface, the mountains of ice ringing it, which, rock as they too are at heart, have fire within, a fire which lifts them endlessly in silent effort toward the darkness above, from which nevertheless comes a dazzling profusion and variety of light, moving or quiet, the sky-spaces of meteor and eclipse. Behind that again looms another and greater universe of being, the world of the apostle's shadow and of communication between the lowlier earth and the towering Forms of more than natural power and place. Then we notice something else: that the poem contains three quotations. The first is: "Where yet the stern and solitary Night / Brook'd no alternate Sway"; the second: "hold the moon and stars in fee"; the third: "Dread ambassadors from earth to Heaven, / Great hierarchs." On first reading this I said to myself, "Milton?" for Numbers One and Three, while Two sounded to me like a ballad; I had "True Thomas" in mind, or something like it. I was completely wrong. The only one that is by Milton is Number Two—from the second "Tetrachordon" sonnet—though it is worth remark that Coleridge has altered the Miltonic balance of "held the sun and moon in fee" to suit his own universe of perpetual night. The first quotation is from one of Coleridge's own poems, one of the "bad" ones, "The Destiny of Nations," begun in 1796 and not published finally until 1817. Of this particular passage in it, Lamb said that it could stand comparison with Milton; John Livingston Lowes makes fun of this in *The Road to Xanadu,* but I find myself standing with Lamb. The third quotation also is Coleridge's own, this time from the "Hymn before Sunrise in the Vale of Chamouni," again not reckoned among Coleridge's better, or even unaided, efforts, since a good deal of it is taken from another writer. It too, however, has its moments. I want, in these three quotations, to emphasize two things. First is the recurrence and, in this late poem, the concentration of the epic and cosmic images in which Coleridge, as we have seen, constantly clothes his thinking and his life. The second is the apparent unanimity of the poems, good or bad, in this respect. It is as if, in this late poem, Coleridge sets resonating all his earlier work as well, so that we glimpse the continuity of the images and of the self-allegorizing which he was carrying on.

The poem, as do the many other similar images from Coleridge we have glanced at, bears out the little prose preface or explication which he gives it. It does look as if self-allegory, whatever we may mean by that term, was the method of the poetry, and so we have a tentative answer to one of the questions we set ourselves earlier. Allegory of the life—but not just of that life in its external happenings, though that too enters in, and sea-metaphors take on a horrid aptness here, for one could well say of Coleridge's life, in this sense, that he made shipwreck of it. Indeed, he says so himself. No, it is allegory also of life at another level, at once more interior and more public. The vision is not only of himself, of S.T.C., or of a soul, *sub specie aeternatis.* It is of the life which he shares, as in our own degree so do we, with those great ones by whom he saw himself surrounded. It is an allegory of the community of energy, thought, hidden volcanic effort, which genius constitutes. The allegory, including the self-allegory, is the way in to the comprehension of this. If self-allegory is the method of the poetry, the poetry in its turn becomes the method by which to penetrate, and unite ourselves with, the life of thought as carried on by others or by ourselves.

What response or clarification to this, if any, can the "Essay on Method" offer? Will the Method which Coleridge sets out to display in his prose works on the subject and which, he insists, is inherent in poetry as well as in science or philosophy or education (he mentions all of these) be able to link up with the Method which the poetry suggests? At this point we had better take up one of our own earlier questions, and ask, in a Coleridgean but also in a wider sense, what Method is.

It is essentially a Method of thinking; and we shall never grasp what that entails if we assume, hard and fast as all of us do, that we know how to think. I would suggest that we do not. (You may discover this, as I did, by trying to think; not just to analyze, combine, order, deduce, which we all know how to do, but to think.) Coleridge says of our proceedings here and our customary ascription to ourselves of the power of thought, that "it is by voluntary negation and act of no thinking that we think. . . ." [7] when we adopt just such unquestioning assumptions. If we can apply this literally, we may begin to grasp what is meant by Method here. Coleridge himself saw it as part of a "general revolution," which he regarded as essential, "in the modes of developing and disciplining the human Mind," [8] words which, if true in his own time, are even more urgent in ours.

Method, which is common to science and literature, has, as Coleridge sets it before us, three parts. These he calls the Initiative, the Progressive Transition, and the Idea or Law, those two terms being here convertible. We will take the beginning and end first.

Of the Initiative we have already seen something, in the passages quoted from the "Essay on Method" and *The Friend,* and in the images by which Coleridge tries to embody this first faculty of thinking, the asking of a "good" question,[9] the query which is forethoughtful, that is, can think forward, which Coleridge also calls a prior purpose, a precogitation, the staple or starting post of a whole train of thought. There is a polar relation (of attraction, which is why I am taking them together) between this Initiative and its destination, the Idea which is also, as we heard Coleridge say, "an experiment realised." Of the Idea, the goal toward which thought and thinker move, he says that it may be clear, or "it may be a mere *instinct,* a vague appetency towards something which the Mind incessantly hunts for, but cannot find, like a name which has escaped our recollection" ("Essay on Method," Section I, Head 11). It is the test by which clues are discovered; and sleepwalking process as it often seems, it requires also, this methodologist tells us, "a constant wakefulness of mind." What we seek for is the Idea which is also a Law, to which hypothesis may lead us, but only under certain conditions: "As little can a true scientific method be grounded on a hypothesis, unless where the hypothesis is an exponential image or picture-language of an idea, which is contained in it more or less clearly, or the symbol of an undiscovered law" (*The Friend,* III, Essay VII). As a comment on the corresponsive relation between hypothesis and that which it seeks to grasp, as also on what Coleridge meant by the extraordinary remark which stands as

7. From *Omniana,* quoted in *Coleridge: Select Poetry and Prose,* ed. Stephen Potter (London, 1962), p. 198.

8. Letter to Wordsworth, May 30, 1815 (*Collected Letters,* IV, 575). The context is interesting, for Coleridge is outlining the vast philosophical poem he is still urging Wordsworth to write.

9. "A good problem is the anticipation of a hidden truth and its clues represent an aspect of the future discovery to be made by solving the problem; to recognise a problem is to discern an aspect of a hidden truth." This is a scientist exploring the same ground—Michael Polanyi in the third of a series of lectures as yet unpublished, entitled "Man in Thought," given at Duke University in 1964.

epigraph to what I am saying here, this passage could hardly be bettered.

Between Initiative and Idea comes Progressive Transition, the dynamic, motion, path, by which the mind finds its way toward its objective, voyaging across chaos, for "all things, in us, and about us, are a Chaos, without Method" ("Essay on Method," Section I, Head 5), and the beginning of getting clear of chaos is, Coleridge says, to observe relations.[10] The path of transition, the unifying principle which is also the innermost activity of the human mind, lies here. He produces, once again, extraordinary images for this aspect of the mind's work or, rather, its life: germinations of the mind; the orbits of thought, as if it were some starry or Miltonic chaos we had to navigate through; the self-observation which is for Coleridge the faculty of reflection itself (see *Aids to Reflection, passim,* and elsewhere) as he describes it, "when I am at once waiting for, watching, and organically constructing and inwardly constructed by, the *Ideas*." [11] Best of all, it seems to me, is the wonderful ambiguous phrase with which one could sum up this aspect of the whole process of methodical thought as Coleridge saw it—"the Method, the self-unravelling clue" (*The Friend,* III, Essay XI) —the clue that unravels itself but unravels also the self of the seeker.

Are we not arrived, after all, at something close to self-allegorizing? It looks as if here, in the Method no less than in the poetry, a kind of self-imaging or mythologizing becomes the method of the Method, the central essence of the human intellect. It is not just that this is Coleridge's individual method. He asserts that it is the nature of Method, of thought itself. There is, in this connection, a most interesting entry in the *Notebooks* for 1803. "Seem to have made up my mind," Coleridge says, (how realistically, for this is the exact sensation of reaching a decision on the deeper matters of one's being) "to write my metaphysical works as *my Life,* or *in* my Life—intermixed with all the other events / or history of the mind and fortunes of S.T.C." [12] That the outer events of a man's life may be myth or allegory was vouched for by Milton and Keats, among others, and toward the end

10. Note the connection of both "chaos" and "relations" with poetry in Coleridge's mind. We have already seen that, for Coleridge, poets "tame the chaos." He also says that the poet, in displaying and unfolding his material, "likewise adds something, namely, light and relations," in *Anima Poetae,* ed. E. H. Coleridge (London, 1895), p. 233.

11. *Inquiring Spirit,* p. 214. He uses the term "self-construction" also; see *Biographia Literaria,* chap. 12, for example. See also chap. 3 of I. A. Richards, *Coleridge on Imagination* (3d. ed.; London, 1962), for a most imaginative and understanding discussion of what Coleridge is doing here.

12. *Notebooks,* I, Entry 1515.

41

of my last book [13] I was trying to work out some of the implications of this. I see now, however, that one must take this further, for here Coleridge introduces a new possibility, the intense life-narrative of the thinking mind (that is, every human mind: "If you are not a *thinking* man, to what purpose are you a *man* at all?" he asks in the Preface to *Aids to Reflection*) claiming, as the external life may also do, epic for its quality and myth for its method.

This is not merely a literary matter; and the limited *Biographia Literaria* becomes here what Coleridge calls, in a letter to the Reverend Edward Coleridge, 1827, "my Biographia Interior." Beyond the method as it relates to the individual lies something else, only just visible. The Coleridgean Method, in prose or poetry, rests in the end on something like a vast simile: thinking is like living, or more like living than anything else, both being serial processes involving the observer and open-ended toward the future. And, taking it the other way about, living or life resembles thinking and so might be imaged as a speculative discipline. (It is a figure which scientists have recently made use of, in a scope that ranges from the embryo and its development to the incursion of novelty into the processes of biological evolution.) Further, we glimpse that this operative simile can be observed only at its image-point, directly only within the self, less directly within the selves of others. There is no thought and no life without its accompanying body or image, in which and as which it appears and can alone be known. Perhaps this is also something of what Coleridge meant by the danger of thinking without images.

This is to wander maybe impermissibly far from a literary, let alone a critical, context. So let me revert to something at least approximately literary by way of conclusion. It is curious that Wordsworth and Coleridge both confront us with the puzzle of great men who set out to write a great work, each his own, and who apparently failed to do so. With Wordsworth it is *The Recluse,* of which we have, essentially, only *The Prelude.* It has been argued, however, that in *The Prelude* he did in fact write that great work which he had set himself, though without realizing it; and with this I would agree. Coleridge meant to write *his* "Great Work," seeing it sometimes as prose, sometimes as poetry; and, again, he apparently did not. But here too perhaps we should take another look. We might at least consider the possibility that he, in his poetry and methodology and the life of his mind—all three being inseparable—did accomplish an extraordinary work, that of extending Method. As Wordsworth extended the epic,

13. *The Human Metaphor* (Notre Dame, 1964).

explicitly, from where Milton had brought it, Coleridge extends Method from the point at which Bacon left it, reinterpreting it now as a power of living, a self-allegorizing, self-constructing power through which all thought, which is to say, all interpretation of the universe, must be carried on. Experiments and extensions in Method always appear rather dark. Even Bacon's Method still remains fragmentary and mysterious in our eyes, if passionately exciting to those who catch anything of it at all, just because so full of futurity, as Coleridge implies when he calls Bacon "that mine of enkindling truths and pregnant expressions," [14] a splendidly mixed metaphor of images of promise awaiting the digging out, the full blaze, the living birth.

It fell to Wordsworth to write a history, in epic terms, of the growth of the mind, a piece of research we cannot be too grateful for. History, though, deals with the past. It seems to me that what Coleridge has hold of, on the other hand, or what has hold of him, is an intimate commitment to the investigation of the prophetic or forward-thinking powers of the human mind, to be explored through the self raised, in the mathematical sense, to the allegorical or mythical power; and this may illuminate the apparently similarly forethoughtful powers of life itself. On either side of this enormous question, almost all work is still to do. It is this commitment, in his true character of poet-methodologist, which makes him, in his own words [15] (though he uses the phrase not of himself but of the human intellect and its powers), "a presence to the future."

14. In a MS (? 1822) giving an "Outline of an Art of Reasoning," quoted in *Coleridge on Logic and Learning*, p. 77.

15. *Lay Sermons: The Statesman's Manual*, ed. Derwent Coleridge (London, 1852), Appendix B, p. 86.

The Critic
as Artist
as Wilde

3

RICHARD ELLMANN

IN 1914 HENRY JAMES could complain that there was not enough criticism about to give novelists their bearings, while T. S. Eliot and Saul Bellow have recently regretted, for different reasons and in different tones of voice, that there is now too much. The obtrusive place of the critic today can be related to a methodological emphasis which is conspicuous in other disciplines as well. But Wilde was one of the first to see that the exaltation of the artist required a concomitant exaltation of the critic. If art was to have a special train, the critic must keep some seats reserved on it.

Wilde reached this conclusion by way of two others. The first is that criticism plays a vital role in the creative process. If this sounds like T. S. Eliot admonishing Matthew Arnold, Wilde had expressed it, also as an admonition to Arnold, almost thirty years before. The

44

second is that criticism is an independent branch of literature with its own procedures. "I am always amused," says Wilde, "by the silly vanity of those writers and artists of our day who seem to imagine that the primary function of the critic is to chatter about their second-rate work." And he complains that "the poor reviewers are apparently reduced to be the reporters of the police-court of literature, the chroniclers of the doings of the habitual criminals of art." In protesting the independence of criticism Wilde sounds like an ancestral Northrop Frye. These portentous comparisons do indeed claim virtue by association, and such a claim can be broadened. André Gide found Nietzsche less exciting because he had read Wilde, and Thomas Mann in one of his last essays remarks with some chagrin on how many of Nietzsche's aphorisms might have been expressed by Wilde, and how many of Wilde's by Nietzsche. What I think can be urged for Wilde, then, is that for his own reasons and in his own way he laid the basis for many critical positions which are still debated in much the same terms, and which we like to attribute to more ponderous names.

When Wilde formulated his theories the public was more hostile to criticism than it is now, and Wilde was flaunting his iconoclasm, his contempt for the unconsidered and so uncritical pieties of his age. This, in fact, was his mode: not to speak for the Victorians, or for the prematurely old writers who dithered that they were the end of an era, as if they must expire with the 1800's. Wilde proposed to speak for the young, with even excessive eagerness. His own age was always a little embarrassing for him, because he had already completed a degree at Trinity College, Dublin when he went up to Oxford. He was not above a little deception on this score. In 1877, when he was twenty-three, he sent a poem to Gladstone with a letter saying, "I am little more than a boy." And in a poem written that year he spoke of his "boyish passion" and described himself as "one who scarce has seen some twenty summers." This line, in turn, he repeated in his poem "The Sphinx," finished when he was forty. Even in court he injudiciously testified that he was two years younger than he was, so that he sounds a little like Falstaff shouting to Bardolph during the robbery, "They hate us youth." Wilde's mode was calculated juvenescence, and the characters in his books are always being warned by shrewder characters of the danger of listening to people older than themselves. To help reduce that danger, Wilde's characters are invariably parentless. The closest kin allowed is an aunt.

Like Stendhal, Wilde thought of himself as a voice of the age to be, rather than of the one that was fading. Yet like anyone else writing criticism in the later nineteenth century, he had to come to terms with the age that had been, and especially with everybody's parent, Matthew Arnold. Wilde sought Arnold's approbation for his first book *Poems* in 1881, which he sent with a letter stressing their shared Oxonian connections. These extended, though he wisely didn't enforce the claim, to their both having won the Newdigate. Actually their prize-winning poems offer a contrast of manners, Arnold's being just as determined to appear older as Wilde's younger than his years. Arnold replied politely.

But by 1881 Arnold was genuinely old, and seven years later, in 1888, he was dead. Wilde's only book of criticism, *Intentions,* was written during the three years following Arnold's death and published in 1891, as if to take over that critical burden and express what Arnold had failed to say. Yeats thought the book "wonderful," and Walter Pater handsomely praised it for carrying on, "more perhaps than any other writer, the brilliant critical work of Matthew Arnold." Pater's encomium is a reminder, however, not to ignore *him.* There are not two but three critical phases in the late nineteenth century, with Pater transitional between Arnold and Wilde.

In 1864, lecturing from the Oxford Chair in Poetry on "The Function of Criticism at the Present Time," Arnold declared—to everyone's lasting memory—that the "aim of criticism is to see the object as in itself it really is." This statement went with his demand for disinterested curiosity as the mark of the critic; its inadvertent effect was to put the critic on his knees before the work he was discussing. Not everyone enjoyed this position. Nine years later Walter Pater wrote his preface to *Studies in the History of the Renaissance.* Pretending to agree with Arnold's definition of the aim of criticism, he quoted it, then added, "And the first step towards seeing one's object as it really is, is to know one's impression as it really is, to discriminate it, to realize it distinctly." But Pater's corollary subtly altered the original proposition; it shifted the center of attention from the rock of the object to the winds of the perceiver's sensations. It made the critic's own work more important as well as more subjective. If observation is still the word, the critic looks within himself as often as out upon the object.

Wilde had been Pater's student, and in *Intentions* eighteen years later he tweaks Arnold's nose with the essay which in its first published form was entitled "The True Function and Value of Criticism, with Some Remarks on the Importance of Doing Nothing." Here Wilde rounded on Arnold by asserting that the aim of criticism is to see the object as it really is not. This might seem to justify the rhapsodical criticism of Ruskin and Pater, and Wilde uses them as examples. His contention goes beyond their practice, however; he wishes to free critics from subordination, to grant them a larger share in the production of literature. While he doesn't forbid them to explain a book, they might prefer, he said, to deepen a book's mystery. (This purpose is amusing but out of date now; who could deepen the mystery of *Finnegans Wake?*) At any rate, their context would be different from that of the creative artist. For just as the artist claimed independence of received experience (Picasso tells us that art is "what nature is not"), so the critic claimed independence of received books. "The highest criticism," according to Wilde, "is the record of one's own soul." More closely he explained that the critic must have all literature in his mind and see particular works in that perspective rather than in isolation. Thus he, and we as well, "shall be able to realize, not merely our own lives, but the collective spirit of the race, and so to make ourselves absolutely modern, in the true meaning of the word modernity. For he to whom the present is the only thing that is present, knows nothing of the age in which he lives. To realize the nineteenth century, one must realize every century that has preceded it and has contributed to its making." Through knowledge the critic might become more creative than the creative artist, a paradox which has been expressed with more solemnity by Norman Podhoretz about literature of the present day.

Wilde reached these formulations of his aesthetic ideas late in his short life. They were latent, however, in his earliest known essay, "The Rise of Historical Criticism," which he wrote as a university exercise. While praising historians for their scrupulousness, Wilde finds the core of history to be the wish not merely to paint a picture, but to investigate laws and tendencies. He celebrates those historians who impose dominion upon fact instead of surrendering to it. Later he was to say much more boldly, "The one duty we owe to history is to rewrite it." It is part of his larger conception that the one duty (or better, whim) we owe nature, reality, or the world, is to reconstruct it.

When Wilde turned to literary as distinguished from historical criticism, he at first was content to follow Pater. Wilde was won by Pater's espousal of gemlike flames and of high temperatures both in words and in life. Next to him Arnold sounded chilly, never so Victorian as when he was cogently criticizing Victorianism. That word "impression," with which Pater sought to unlock everything, became a favorite word in both Wilde and later in Arthur Symons, and was only arrested by Yeats in the late 1890's because he could not bear so much impermanence and insisted on a metaphysical basis—the *Anima Mundi*—for transitory moods. Like the word "absurd" today, though without a systematic philosophy behind it, the word "impression" agitated against pat assumptions and preconceptions.

Pater's vocabulary shapes the initial poem of Wilde's book of verse, published when he was twenty-five. This poem, "Hélas!," encapsulates much of Wilde's temperament, but with Pater's coloring:

> To drift with every passion till my soul
> Is a stringed lute on which all winds can play,
> Is it for this that I have given away
> Mine ancient wisdom, and austere control?
> Methinks my life is a twice-written scroll
> Scrawled over on some boyish holiday
> With idle songs for pipe and virelay
> Which do but mar the secret of the whole.
> Surely there was a time I might have trod
> The sunlit heights, and from life's dissonance
> Struck one clear chord to reach the ears of God:
> Is that time dead? lo! with a little rod
> I did but touch the honey of romance—
> And must I lose a soul's inheritance?

To call the poem "Hélas!," to sigh in a foreign language, alerts us that the confession to follow will luxuriate in its penitence. The biblical archaisms which occur later offer compunction suitably perfumed. "To drift" may well put us off as weak; on the other hand, to drift with every passion is not so bad. As its image of passivity the poem offers "a stringed lute upon which all winds can play." For the romantic the Aeolian harp was a favorable image because it harmonized man and nature. Here the winds are winds of temptation, rather than gusts of Lake Country air. The rhetorical question which begins, "Is it for this?" sounds reproachful enough, yet the phrases "ancient wisdom" and "austere control"—self-congratulatory since Wilde never had either—are so vague as to constitute a stately but equally unenergetic alternative to drifting.

The word "drift" comes down from Oxford in the 1870's. It occupies a prominent position in Pater's *Studies in the History of the Renaissance,* and specifically in the notorious conclusion to that book. This "Conclusion" was included in the edition of 1873, but omitted in 1877, when Wilde was Pater's student, on the ground that it "might possibly mislead" the young, who accordingly thronged to be misled by the first edition. It was the boldest thing Pater ever wrote; he drew upon the scientific work of his day to deny the integrity of objects. Physical life is now recognized, he says, to be a concurrence of forces

48

rather than a group of things; the mind has no fixities either. He hits upon a metaphor of liquidity such as William James and Bergson were to adopt a little later in characterizing consciousness as a river or stream; Pater says more balefully that consciousness is a whirlpool, an image which later both Yeats and Pound relished. In our physical life, Pater grants, we sometimes feel momentarily at rest; in our consciousness, however, altering the whirlpool image, he finds "nothing but the race of the mid-stream, a drift of momentary acts of sight and passion and thought." To drift is not so wanton, then, as inevitable. To guide our drifting we should rely not on sights or thoughts, in Pater's view, but on "great passions." "Only be sure it is passion," he puts in as a caveat. He urges his readers to recognize that "not the fruit of experience, but experience itself, is the goal." "Our one hope lies in getting as many pulsations as possible into the given time." This attempt to render experience in terms of quantitatively measurable pulsations sounds a little like *Principles of Literary Criticism*, but Pater's tone is not like Richards'; he plays on the flute for the young to follow him.

When Pater at last decided to reprint this "Conclusion" (in 1888), he toned it down a little. In *Marius the Epicurean* (1885), also later, the word "drift" is again prominent, but this time it is pejorative instead of merely descriptive. To suit his later and more decorous manner Pater, in reviewing *The Picture of Dorian Gray*, complained of the book's "dainty Epicurean theory" because, he said, "A true Epicureanism aims at a complete though harmonious development of man's entire organism. To lose the moral sense therefore, for instance, the sense of sin and righteousness, . . . is to lose, or lower, organisation, to become less complex, to pass from a higher to a lower degree of development." The letting-go, as well as the drawing-back, of Pater are both evident in Wilde. His work celebrates both impulses, balancing or disporting with them. In a letter of March, 1877, written four years before "Hélas!," he informs an Oxford friend:

> I have got rather keen on Masonry lately and believe in it awfully—in fact would be awfully sorry to have to give it up in case I secede from the Protestant Heresy. I now breakfast with Father Parkinson, go to St Aloysius, talk sentimental religion to Dunlop and altogether am caught in the fowler's snare, in the wiles of the Scarlet Woman—I may go over in the vac. [to Catholicism]. I have dreams of a visit to Newman, of the holy sacrament in a new Church, and of a quiet and peace afterwards in my soul. I need not say, though, that I shift with every breath of thought and am weaker and more self-deceiving than ever.

If I *could hope* that the Church would wake in me some earnestness and purity I would go over *as a luxury,* if for no better reason. But I can hardly hope it would, and to go over to Rome would be to sacrifice and give up my two great gods "Money and Ambition."

In this letter Wilde testifies playfully to the same yearning to be earnest that he shows in "Hélas!" and then mocks in his later comedy. He is half converted to Catholicism, half to Masonry. That these two groups cannot bear each other does not prevent their being equally attractive to him; they have parity as new areas of sensation, to be enjoyed wilfully and passingly. If, as Wilde announced later, "The best way to resist temptation is to yield to it," the reason is that having done so one may pass on to the next and the next, and in this concourse one may keep a residual freedom by not lingering with any single temptation long.

During the four years between writing this letter and writing "Hélas!," Wilde had put aside both Catholicism and Masonry. In his sonnet he has in mind chiefly his classical education as contrasted with his romantic self-indulgence. A classicist by training, Wilde considered Hellenism to be the more basic side of his nature, overlaid, but only as a palimpsest conceals the original, by a more modern mode. He berates himself, gently. His new life is made up of "idle songs for pipe and virelay," a self-accusation which only concedes frivolity, not depravity. Moreover, it is artistic frivolity, a further mitigation. Wilde remembered Pater's comment, in the same "Conclusion," that "the wisest" instead of living spend their lives in "art and song." If it is wrong to drift, and Wilde hedges a little, then it is less wrong to drift gracefully. A "boyish holiday" is also not the most offensive way to spend one's time, especially if one likes boys.

The sestet of the poem restates the issue, with new dashes of metaphor. The poet then asks histrionically, "Is that time dead?" He won't say for sure, but again he sweetens his offense: he has but touched with a little rod the honey of romance. The last question is not so much despairing as hopeful. Wilde felt he was superior to both classical and romantic modes, because he could manipulate both: he said in his essay on "The English Renaissance" that this was the strength of the new movement in letters to which he belonged. He thought he had physiological as well as artistic support for this method, because "the desire of any very intensified emotion [is] to be relieved by some emotion that is its opposite." He shifts therefore from foot to foot in other poems besides "Hélas!" "The Sphinx" begins with a fascinated invocation of the sphinx and ends with a strident rejection of her. Wilde summarizes his state or rather his flow of mind in a letter.

> Sometime you will find, even as I have found, that there is no such thing as a romantic experience; there are romantic memories, and there is the desire of romance—that is all. Our most fiery moments of ecstasy are merely shadows of what somewhere else we have felt, or of what we long some day to feel. So at least it seems to me. And, strangely enough, what comes of all this is a curious mixture of ardour and of indifference. I myself would sacrifice everything for a new experience, and I know there is no such thing as a new experience at all. I think I would more readily die for what I do not believe in than for what I hold to be true. I would go to the stake for a sensation and be a sceptic to the last! Only one thing remains infinitely fascinating to me, the mystery of moods. To be master of these moods is exquisite, to be mastered by them more exquisite still. Sometimes I think that the artistic life is a long and lovely suicide, and am not sorry that it is so.

Life then is a willed deliquescence, or more exactly, a progressive surrender of the self to all the temptations appropriate to it.

What Wilde needed was not to avoid the precious occasions of evil in "Hélas!" but to approach more enterprising ones. Yet after his *Poems* appeared in 1881 he was at check for almost six years. He kept busy, he went on a lecture tour for a whole year to America, he returned to England and went lecturing on; he tried unsuccessfully for a post as school inspector such as Matthew Arnold had; erratically still, he married in 1884 and took up husbanding, begetting two children born in 1885 and 1886. Then in 1887 Wilde began the publications by which he is known. He wrote a volume of stories and one of fairy tales, then one of criticism, then five plays, besides editing from 1887 to 1889 a magazine, *Woman's World*—a patrician equivalent of the A & P *Woman's Day*. It would seem that something roused him from the pseudo-consolidation of marriage and lectures, which were dilettantism for him, to genuine consolidation which seemed dilettantism to others.

This something appears in the original version of *The Picture of Dorian Gray*, published in *Lippincott's Magazine*. Wilde emphasizes more there than in the final version the murder of the painter Basil Hallward by Dorian; it is the turning point in Dorian's experience, a plunge from insinuations of criminal tendency to crime itself. The murder at once protects the secret of his double life and vents his revulsion against the man who wants him innocent still. In *Lippincott's* Wilde specifies, "It was on the 7th of November, the eve of his own thirty-second birthday, as he often remembered afterwards. . . ."

Then when the novel was republished as a book, Wilde altered this date: "It was on the ninth of November, the eve of his own thirty-eighth birthday, as he often remembered afterwards."

Altering Dorian's age would be gratuitous if Wilde had not attached significance to his own thirty-second birthday in 1886. The passage must have been autobiographical, and such a conjecture receives support from Robert Ross, who boasted that it was he, at the age of seventeen, who in the year 1886 first seduced Wilde to homosexual practices. Wilde evidently considered this sudden alteration of his life a pivotal matter, to be recast as Dorian's murder of Hallward. He himself moved from pasteboard marriage to the expression of long latent proclivities, at some remove from the "ancient wisdom" and "austere control" to which he had earlier laid claim as his basic nature. Respectability, always an enemy, was destroyed in his own house. The first work which came out of the new Wilde was, appropriately, "Lord Arthur Savile's Crime," in which murder is comically enacted and successfully concealed.

From late in the year 1886 then, Wilde was able to think of himself, if he wanted to, as criminal. Up to that time he could always consider himself an innocent misunderstood; now he lived in such a way as to confirm suspicions. Instead of challenging Victorian society only by words, he acted in such a way as to create scandal. Indiscreet by nature, he was indiscreet also by conviction, and he waged his war somewhat openly. He sensed that his new life was a source of literary effect. As he wrote later of Thomas Wainewright, "His crimes seem to have had an important effect upon his art. They gave a strong personality to his style, a quality that his early work certainly lacked." He returned to this idea, "One can fancy an intense personality being created out of sin," and in "The Soul of Man Under Socialism," he thought that "Crime . . . under certain conditions, may be said to have created individualism." In "The Portrait of Mr. W. H." (1889), he made Shakespeare's *Sonnets* depend upon a similarly forbidden love affair, with the boy actor Willie Hughes. Thomas Mann's Tonio Kröger speaks of a banker who discovers his literary talent by committing a serious crime for which he is put in prison. The artist-criminal is implicit in romantic and symbolistic theories of art, but Wilde anticipates the explicitness of both Mann and Gide on this subject. He might have discounted the sinfulness of his conduct, and applied to himself his own epigram, "Wickedness is a myth invented by good people to account for the curious attractiveness of others." But he was quite content to think of himself as sinful.

He now succeeded in relating his new discoveries about himself to aesthetic theory. His only formal book of criticism, *Intentions,* has the same secret spring as his later plays and stories. Ostensibly, he generally says that the spheres of art and of ethics are absolutely distinct and separate. But occasionally, overtly or covertly, he states that for the artist crime does pay, by instilling itself in his content and affecting his form. Each of the four essays that make up *Intentions* is to some degree subversive, as if to demonstrate that the intentions of the artist are not strictly honorable. The first and the last, "The Decay of Lying" and "The Truth of Masks," celebrate art for rejecting truths, faces, and all that paraphernalia in favor of lies and masks. Wilde doesn't do this in the romantic way of extolling the imagination, for while he uses that word he is a little chary of it; the imagination is itself too natural, too involuntary, for his view of art. He prefers lying because it sounds more wilful, because it is no outpouring of the self, but a conscious effort to mislead. "All fine imaginative work," Wilde affirms, "is self-conscious and deliberate. A great poet sings because he chooses to sing." On the other hand, "if one tells the truth, one is sure, sooner or later, to be found out!" "All bad poetry springs from genuine feeling." Wilde celebrates art not in the name of Ariel, as the romantics would, but in the name of Ananias.

He finds art to have two basic energies, both of them subversive. One asserts its magnificent isolation from experience, its unreality, its sterility. He would concur with Nabokov that art is a kind of trick played on nature, an *illicit* creation by man. "All art is entirely useless," Wilde declares. "Art never expresses anything but itself." "Nothing that actually occurs is of the smallest importance." Form determines content, not content form, a point which Auden also sometimes affirms and which is often assumed by symbolists. With this theory Wilde turns Taine upon his head; the age does not determine what its art should be, rather it is art which gives the age its character. So far from responding to questions posed by the epoch, art offers answers before questions have been asked. "It is the ages that are her symbols." Life, straggling after art, seizes upon forms in art to express itself, so that life imitates art rather than art life. ". . . This unfortunate aphorism about Art holding the mirror up to Nature, is," according to Wilde, "deliberately said by Hamlet in order to convince the bystanders of his absolute insanity in all art-matters." If art be a mirror, we look into it to see—a mask. But more precisely, art is no mirror; it is a "mist of words," "a veil."

Sometimes the veil is pierced. This indifferent conferral of forms upon life by art may have unexpected consequences which implicate art instead of isolating it. In "The Decay of Lying" Wilde speaks of "silly boys who, after reading the adventures of Jack Sheppard or Dick Turpin, pillage the stalls of unfortunate applewomen, break into sweetshops at night, and alarm old gentlemen who are returning home from the city by leaping out on them in suburban lanes, with black masks and unloaded revolvers." In *Dorian Gray* the effect is more sinister; Dorian declares he has been poisoned by a book, and while Lord Henry assures him that art is too aloof to influence anybody, Dorian is felt to be right. Art may then transmit criminal impulses to its audience. Like Whitman, Wilde could and did say, "Nor will my poems do good only, they will do just as much evil, perhaps more."

The artist may be criminal and instill his work with criminality. Wilde's second essay in *Intentions* is "Pen, Pencil and Poison." He uses Thomas Wainewright as the type of the artist. We need not expect to find a beautiful soul; Wainewright was instead "a forger of no mean capabilities, and . . . a subtle and secret poisoner almost without rival in this or any age." Among his interesting tastes, Wainewright had "that curious love of green, which in individuals is always the sign of a subtle artistic temperament, and in nations is said to denote a laxity, if not a decadence of morals." When a friend reproached him with a murder, he shrugged his shoulders and gave an answer that Susan Sontag would call "camp": "Yes; it was a dreadful thing to do, but she had very thick ankles." Wilde concludes that "the fact of a man being a poisoner is nothing against his prose," and "there is no essential incongruity between crime and culture." Wainewright's criminal career turns out to be strictly relevant to his art, fortifying it and giving it character. The quality of that art is too early to judge, Wilde says, but he clearly believes that Wainewright's personality achieves sufficient criminality to have great artistic promise.

"The Critic as Artist" is the most ambitious of the essays in *Intentions*. It too conveys the notion that art undermines things as they are. The critic is the artist's accomplice in crime, or even masterminds the plot in which they are mutually engaged. Criticism overcomes the tendency of creation to repeat itself; it helps the artist discover unused possibilities. For at bottom, Wilde says, criticism is self-consciousness; it enables us to put our most recent phase at a distance and so go on to another. It disengages us so we may re-engage ourselves in a new way.

From this argument Wilde proceeds to find criticism and self-consciousness to be as necessary as sin. "What is termed Sin is an essential element of progress"; without it, he holds, the world would stagnate or grow old or become colorless. "By its curiosity [there is

Arnold's word with Wilde's meaning] Sin increases the experience of the race. Through its intensified assertion of individualism it saves us from monotony of type. In its rejection of the current notions about morality, it is one with the highest ethics." By a dexterous transvaluation of words, Wilde makes good and evil exchange places. Even socially, sin is far more useful than martyrdom, he says, since it is self-expressive rather than self-repressive. The goal of man is the liberation of personality; when the day of true culture comes, sin will be impossible because the soul will be able to transform "into elements of a richer experience, or a finer susceptibility, or a newer mode of thought, acts or passions that with the common would be commonplace, or with the uneducated ignoble, or with the shameful vile. Is this dangerous? Yes; it is dangerous—all ideas, as I told you, are so." What muddies this point of view in Wilde is his clinging to conventional meanings of words like "sin," "ignoble," and "shameful." He is not so ready as Nietzsche to transvaluate these, although he does reshuffle them. His private equation is that sin is the perception of new and dangerous possibilities in action as self-consciousness is in thought and criticism is in art. He espouses individualism, and he encourages society to make individualism more complete than it can be now, and for this reason he sponsors socialism as a communal egotism, like the society made up of separate but equal works of art.

Meantime, before socialism, what should be thought of the criminal impulses of the artist? Increasingly in his later writings, Wilde spreads the guilt from the artist to all men. If we are all insincere, masked, and lying, then the artist is prototype rather than exception. If all the sheep are black, then the artist can't be blamed for not being white. Such an exculpation is implied in three of Wilde's plays after *Salomé*—*Lady Windermere's Fan, A Woman of No Importance, An Ideal Husband.* Wilde allows his characters to be found guilty, but no guiltier than others, and more courageous in their wrongdoing.

While defending them, he allows them to be mildly punished. Half-consciously, he was preparing himself for another abrupt shift in his experience, such as he had made in 1886. It would be false to say that Wilde wanted to go to prison, yet the notion had frequently crossed his mind. He had always associated himself with the *poètes maudits,* always considered obloquy a certificate of literary merit. In "The Soul of Man Under Socialism" he had opposed suffering, yet acknowledged that the Russian novelists had rediscovered a great medieval theme, the realization of man through suffering. More particularly, in a review of a new book of poems by Wilfred Scawen Blunt in

1889, he began, "Prison has had an admirable effect on Mr. Wilfred Blunt as a poet." It was like the effect of crime on Wainewright. Blunt had been merely witty and affected earlier, now his work had more depth. "Mr. Balfour must be praised," Wilde says jestingly, since "by sending Mr. Blunt to gaol . . . [he] has converted a clever rhymer into an earnest and deep-thinking poet." Six years later, just before his own disgrace, Wilde wrote in "The Soul of Man under Socialism," "After all, even in prison a man can be quite free." These hints indicate that Wilde was prepared, or thought he was, for trial and prison, and expected he would derive artistic profit from them. He had no idea of running away, even on a boyish holiday, whatever his friends might say. Instead he accepted imperial authority as readily as Christ had done—a precedent he discovered for himself, though hardly the first or last in hot water to do so. Blunt's poems written in prison were called *In Vinculis,* and Wilde's letter to Douglas from prison, which we know by Ross's title as *De Profundis,* was originally entitled by Wilde *Epistola: In Carcere et Vinculis.*

Hélas! Wilde's literary career was not transmogrified by prison as he hoped, but his experiences there, which were so much worse than he anticipated, gave him his final theme. As before, he made no effort to exonerate himself by saying that his sins were venial or not sins at all. Defenses of homosexuality or "Uranian" love were common enough at this period; he did not make them. But he reached for the main implication of his disgrace through a double negative; though men thought he was unlike them, he was *not.* He was a genuine scapegoat.

This ultimate conception of himself was never put into an essay, but it is involved in his *De Profundis* letter to Douglas, and in the "The Ballad of Reading Gaol." Both are predictably full of imagery of Christ. Before this Wilde had depreciated pity as a motive in art; now he embraced it. The hero of his poem is a man who has murdered his mistress and is about to be hanged for his crime. Wilde identifies himself closely with this prisoner. The poem's tenor is that the prisoners are humanity, all of whom are felons:

> Yet each man kills the thing he loves,
>   By each let this be heard,
> Some do it with a bitter look,
>   Some with a flattering word,
> The coward does it with a kiss,
>   The brave man with a sword!
>
>   .   .   .   .

56

Some love too little, some too long,
   Some sell, and others buy;
Some do the deed with many tears,
   And some without a sigh:
For each man kills the thing he loves,
   Yet each man does not die.

This poem was chosen for *The Oxford Book of Modern Verse* by Yeats, but he removed what he regarded as the commentary, including these stanzas. His effort to improve the poem evokes sympathy; it must be said, however, that whatever the quality of the bare narrative that Yeats prints, for Wilde—as for D. H. Lawrence and most readers—the commentary was the excessive and yet telling part of the poem. During the six years before his imprisonment he had demonstrated first that the artist was basically and usefully criminal, and second that criminality was not confined to artists, but was to be found as commonly among members of the Cabinet. Where most men pretend to a virtue they don't have, the artist, fully aware of his own sins, takes on those they don't acknowledge. The purpose of sin has subtly shifted in Wilde's mind: it is no longer a means for the artist of extending the boundaries of action, it is a means for him to focus and monopolize guilt. He has the courage, exceptional among men, of looking into the heart of things and finding there not brotherly love so much as murder, not self-love so much as suicide. In recognizing the universality of guilt he is like Christ; in revealing his own culpability he plays the role of his own Judas. Wilde, who had written in one of his poems that we are ourselves "the lips betraying and the life betrayed," had in fact brought about his own conviction. The result was that he was remarried to the society from which he had divorced himself; he was no outcast, for he accepted and even sought the punishment which other men, equally guilty, would only submit to vicariously through him, just as all the prisoners suffer with the doomed murderer. By means of submission and suffering he gives his life a new purpose, and writes over the palimpsest once again.

In this concern with social role Wilde has clearly moved away from Pater, and perhaps we can conceive of him as moving toward another writer, Jean Genet. Genet is of course ferocious and remorseless in a way that Wilde was not, and makes much less concession to the world. But the two men share an insistence on their own criminality and on a possible sanction for it. The comparison with Christ has been irresistible for both. As Genet says in *Thief's Journal,* "Let us ignore the theologians. 'Taking upon Himself the sins of the world' means exactly this: experiencing potentially and in their effects all sins; it means having subscribed to evil. Every creator must thus shoulder— the expression seems feeble—must make his own, to the point of knowing it to be his substance, circulating in his arteries, the evil given by him, which his heroes choose freely." And again, Genet speaks like Wilde of the courage required to do wrong, saying, "If he has courage, the guilty man decides to be what crime has made him." He wishes to obtain "the recognition of evil." Both writers envisage a regeneration which can come only from total assumption of their proclivities and their lot; as Genet puts it, "I shall destroy appearances, the casings will burn away and one evening I shall appear there, in the palm of your hand, quiet and pure, like a glass statuette. You will see me. Round about me there will be nothing left." Wilde summons for this sacred moment a red rose growing from the hanged man's mouth, a white one from his heart. He had terrified André Gide by trying to persuade that strictly reared young man to authorize evil, as to some extent in the *acte gratuit* Gide did, and it is just such authorization that Genet asserts with more fierceness than Wilde.

In his criticism and in his work generally, Wilde balanced two ideas which, we have observed, look contradictory. One is that art is disengaged from actual life, the other that it is deeply incriminated with it. The first point of view is sometimes taken by Yeats, though only to qualify it; the second without qualification by Genet. That art is sterile, or that it is infectious, are attitudes not beyond reconciliation. Wilde never formulated their union, but he implied something like this: by its creation of beauty art reproaches the world, calling attention to the world's faults by their very omission; so the sterility of art is an affront or a parable. Art may also outrage the world by flouting its laws or by picturing indulgently their violation. Or art may seduce the world by making it follow an example which seems bad but is discovered to be better than it seems. In these various ways the artist forces the world towards self-recognition, with at least a tinge of self-redemption.

Yet this ethical or almost ethical view of art coexists in Wilde with its own cancellation. He could write *Salomé* with one hand, dwelling upon incest and necrophilia, and show them as self-defeated, punished by execution and remorse. With the other hand, he could dissolve by the critical intellect all notions of sin and guilt. He does so in *The Importance of Being Earnest*, which is all insouciance where *Salomé* is all incrimination. In *The Importance of Being Earnest* sins which are presented as accursed in *Salomé* and unnamable in *Dorian Gray* are translated into a different key. They appear as Algernon's inordinate and selfish craving for—cucumber sandwiches. The substitution of mild gluttony for fearsome lechery renders all vice harmless. There *is* a wicked brother, but he is just our old friend Algernon. The double life which is so serious a matter for Dorian or for The Ideal Husband, becomes a harmless Bunburying, or playing Jack in the country and Ernest in town. In the earlier, four-act version of the play, Wilde even parodied punishment, by having a bailiff come to take Jack to Holloway Prison, not for homosexuality, but for running up food bills at the Savoy. Jack is disinclined, he says, to be imprisoned in the suburbs for dining in town, and makes out a cheque. The notion of expiation is also mocked; as Cecily says: "They have been eating muffins. That looks like repentance." Finally, the theme of regeneration is parodied in the efforts of Ernest and Jack to be baptized. (By the way, in the earlier version Prism is also about to be baptized, and someone comments, "To be born again would be of considerable advantage to her.") The ceremonial unmasking at the play's end, which had meant death for Dorian Gray, leaves everyone barefaced for a new puppet show, that of matrimony. Yet amusing as it all is, much of the comedy derives from Wilde's own sense of the realities of what are being mocked. He was in only momentary refuge from his more usual cycle which ran from scapegrace to scapegoat.

During his stay in prison Wilde took up the regeneration theme in *De Profundis* and after being freed he resumed it in "The Ballad of Reading Gaol." But he was too self-critical not to find the notion of rebirth a little preposterous. When his friends complained of his resuming old habits, he said, "A patriot put in prison for loving his country loves his country, and a poet in prison for loving boys loves boys." But to write about himself as unredeemed, unpunished, unreborn, to claim that his sins were nothing, that his form of love was more noble than most other people's, that what had happened to him was the result merely of legal obtuseness, was impossible for Wilde. So long as he had been a scapegrace the door to comedy was still open; once having accepted the role of scapegoat the door was closed. He conceived of a new play, but it was in his earlier mode and he could not write it. Cramped to one myth, and that sombre and depleted, Wilde could not extricate himself. There was nothing to do but die, which accordingly he did. But not without one final assertion of a past enthusiasm: he was converted to Catholicism the night before his death.

NOTE: Quotations from letters are taken from *The Letters of Oscar Wilde*, ed. Rupert Hart-Davis (London and New York, 1962).

Wallace Stevens and Rainer Maria Rilke: Two Versions of a Poetic

4

RALPH FREEDMAN

· 1 ·

THE SUBJECT to which we have been asked to address ourselves—the aesthetic of poets in their poetry—is illuminated sharply, if self-consciously, by Rainer Maria Rilke and Wallace Stevens, aesthetic poets indeed. But a glance suggests that our subject at once invites a larger one. It raises the vexing question of philosophical poetry in general, for if we say that a poem expresses an aesthetic, it is almost the same as saying that ideas are apprehended and exist in its rhetoric or images. When Wallace Stevens writes in his essay "A Collect of Philosophy" that "the idea of infinity of the world is a poetic idea, because it gives the imagination sudden life," [1] he clearly states an aesthetic, because he tries to define what a poetic idea is. At

1. *Opus Posthumous* (New York, 1957) , p. 183.

the same time, he also raises a larger question about the meaning of infinity, of our knowing that which is infinite as a philosophical or poetic enterprise, and the relationship of the capabilities of our knowledge to that which is ordinarily knowable and that which is not. If now we translate this kind of question from prose into verse, we see that here, too, our means of awareness involve an aesthetic and a general philosophy as well. Rilke's and Stevens' poetics involve such a view of poetry as an embodiment and immediate presentation of knowledge. They are both "philosophical poets."

If it were not for this connection, any comparison of Rilke and Stevens, as poets or as aestheticians, would seem either fortuitous or academic. Their similarities appear to be largely external: they both wrote a great deal of obscure poetry and used painting and music for their subjects. Born in the same decade—Rilke in 1875, Stevens in 1879—they were formed by the pieties and apostasies of an identical generation. Thus both admired Baudelaire and the French *fin de siècle*, tried to come to terms with science and psychology, absorbed Cézanne and the Post-Impressionists, were involved in experiments with language. Stevens shared Rilke's preoccupation with things which he had found among the Imagists, certainly in Marianne Moore whom he admired. And Rilke had influenced the Imagist Movement. On the other hand, Stevens' thrust reaches farther into our own time, for Rilke died in 1926, only three years after the publication of *Harmonium*, while Stevens lived until 1955. He therefore could press his use of pictorial composition beyond Cézanne to the late Picasso and observe the shift in literary sensibility that turned the avant-gardists of Rilke's time—Mallarmé, Pound, Eliot, Rilke himself—into a new establishment. And finally, while they were separated by a gulf in national traditions—Stevens' America, in which he felt deeply rooted, was for Rilke a real mechanistic evil—they shared similar intellectual roots, because they both turned to France for aesthetic nourishment.

But all these matters are on the surface. A vast chasm of tone divides the two poets. There is a fleshly substance to Stevens, a disdain for that very sentiment at which Rilke was dangerously adept. Rilke's work may be more varied in its themes and more comprehensive in its methods, but Stevens' ironic stance he seldom mastered; light wit does not occur often in his verse, which remains evanescent, lofty, yet rarely unengaged. Precisely for this reason, however, Stevens is more unapproachable. There is in his poems little of that quality which Thomas Mann called "cow warmth," in both of its intended meanings of ironic deprecation and human need; Stevens' poetry does not share Rilke's imploring gestures. It has been said of Stevens that while love was often his subject, he seldom wrote love poems. Rilke always wrote love poems, even at his most abstract, as he always wrote love letters, intense, tender, whether to women, to poets, or to God. Stevens' wit and detachment, then, stand out distinctly when reflected against Rilke's gentle, often even sentimental tone.

The grounds for our comparison, then, are given by the task we have set ourselves: to explore two versions of a poetic in Stevens' and Rilke's verse. In the light of this excursion, their concern with the conditions of poetic knowledge becomes more than a superficial fact. And in this connection, a particular involvement in painting—its special manner of seeing which the two poets shared—becomes a crucial point of comparison. For both poets insisted with remarkable intensity, almost with jealousy, on penetrating behind the painter's eye. This passion to adopt another art form can, of course, be historically explained as a mutually shared tradition which emanated from Poe and Baudelaire and has communicated itself to the twentieth century through the Symbolist experiment. But to say this is not quite saying enough, because the two poets partake not only of a general theory about the interrelation of the arts, but also of a virtual obsession with the way artists see things. Indeed, the largest common ground for their poetic is described by this need to see, through the painter's or sculptor's eye, how objects blend with and dissolve into space, how they become something other than themselves, how, with their particular vision, painters confer life upon matter. In the concluding lines of a small poem from *New Poems*, "The Unicorn," Rilke both renders and dissolves a heraldic figure:

Das Maul mit seinem rosagrauen Flaum
was leicht gerafft, so dass ein wenig Weiss
(weisser als alles) von den Zähnen glänzte;
die Nüstern nahmen auf und lechzten leis.
Doch seine Blicke, die kein Ding begrenzte,
warfen sich Bilder in den Raum
und schlossen einen blauen Sagenkreis.[2]

Mouth curled lightly
with rose-gray down, so that a little white of its teeth
(whiter than everything) gleamed;
nostrils breathing in, languishing softly.
But its eyes, unlimited by any outside thing
cast images into space
and closed a blue mythic circle.

2. *Sämtliche Werke*, ed. Ernst Zinn (Frankfurt, 1955), I, 507. (Hereafter cited as *S.W.*)

The unicorn, rendered through its life and especially its colors (rose-gray and white) becomes itself a cause of seeing as it closes a "blue" mythic circle. Sight projected from the beholder onto the figure of the unicorn turns into an imaginative vision, sight turning into an awareness beyond sight. But at the same time, this penetration of the figure to a realm beyond sense is proof of its own nature as a heraldic representation.

Stevens, when he imitates paintings, is more abstract than Rilke, his patterns more decomposed. The opening lines of a poem entitled "Woman Looking at a Vase of Flowers" at first suppress the main figure entirely:

> It was as if thunder took form upon
> The piano, that time: the time when the crude
> And jealous grandeurs of sun and sky
> Scattered themselves in the garden, like
> The wind dissolving into birds,
> The clouds becoming braided girls.
> It was like the sea poured out again
> In east wind beating the shutters at night.

In the following stanza, Stevens, like Rilke, shows the woman through her activity of seeing:

> Hoot, little owl within her, how
> High blue became particular
> In the leaf and bud and how the red
> Flicked into pieces, points of air,
> Became—how the central, essential red
> Escaped its large abstraction, became,
> First, summer, then a lesser time,
> Then the sides of peaches, of dusky pears.[3]

The figure is shown in her absence, although her presence is felt not only through her sight but also through the imaginative apprehension, her way (with the "little owl within her") of placing "high blue" within leaf and bud. This pattern is decomposed, because the poet also presents the figure as a perceiver and an imagining sensibility which, like Rilke's unicorn, ultimately recreates the woman's essential persona.

If we start out from these two examples of Rilke's and Stevens' verse, and move beyond a strict preoccupation with paintings (a symptom, after all, rather than a pervasive tendency in their work), we shall encounter a similar poetic. Both poets adopted striking positions

3. *Collected Poems* (New York, 1954), p. 246. (Hereafter cited as *C.P.*)

toward their objects, for both saw objects simultaneously as they are and as they are not, through that which is given in perception and that which appears to lie beyond it. Like Baudelaire and Mallarmé before them, they sought metaphysical through epistemological understanding while maintaining the posture of confrontation implicit in the act of knowledge. This stance may be traditional for poets who share the "heritage of Symbolism," but Stevens and Rilke, each in his own way, practiced a unique variation. For unlike T. S. Eliot, for example, each was *unsure* of the relationship between object and knower, as he was *unsure* of the identity of either object or subject, thing or mind, the active or the passive condition. From this insecurity there emerged a rich aesthetic based alike on infinite variations of the theme of knowledge and a comprehensive, if also uncertain, view of the scope and function of the poetic imagination. Stevens' "realistic oreole," as Northrop Frye called it,[4] is given an added dimension through an examination of Rilke's verse, for both poets showed with fascinating versatility how objects relate to minds in the reciprocal tensions of poetry.

· 2 ·

"To exist," wrote Georges Poulet in *Studies in Human Time*, "is to be one's present, and also to be one's past and one's recollections." [5] In relation to the self, this phrase contains each of the elements that defines Wallace Stevens' ambivalence. Existence is first given by itself: one is one's present; objects, sensations, impinge upon one's sight. It is also given in the second instance: one is defined by one's previous states, objects and sensations having impinged upon one's mind in the past. And it is finally rendered in our recollections— our awareness of past states—which supply that consciousness which gives us, and our feelings about things, its specific hue, its tone, its sense of life. Poulet suggested in this passage that these three elements form a unity, but for Stevens they supply at least two different kinds of existence: the self as object in the first and second senses of the quoted phrase, and the self as subject in the third. It is not only upon the latter, but also upon the former that his concept of imagination dwells.

The identical ambivalence exists in relation to the object. We may

4. "The Realistic Oriole: A Study of Wallace Stevens," *Hudson Review*, X (Autumn, 1957), 353–70.
5. *Studies in Human Time*, trans. Elliot Coleman (Baltimore, 1956), p. 24.

assume the stance of the passive experiencer who takes in objects or sensations from the external world and remolds them into a more universal vision within our conscious, or imaginative, experience, to create a metaphysical vision, a manifestation of the spirit, or a work of art. Or we may assume a different position and see the object as distinct from the self, as something external with which the self must come to terms. In this instance, it is the poet's task to give a true picture of the thing as it is, to render it in its purity without any degrading alloys or philistine embellishments. T. E. Hulme associated the first with imagination, the second with fancy, but we might, with Stevens, remain with the term *imagination,* for both describe how words and the mental fictions they create mediate between the conscious poet and the world around him.[6] The first type of imagination, however, we might call an "idealistic" one, not only in the sense of the Romantics but especially in that of *fin de siècle* poetics. The second we might call "realistic." Both are traditional terms in philosophy as well as in aesthetics, and both depend upon the poet's eye to lead us safely from one kind of understanding to the other.

For Stevens, there was no clear choice between these two types of the imagination. Although he wrote frequently about *imagination* as a term, both theories we have described entered his poems simultaneously as well as on different occasions. Our example of "The Woman Looking at a Vase of Flowers" has shown how a subject can be dissolved through the manner in which it is seen and how, in the second stanza, the flowers themselves drew the contours of the imaginative act (through their particulars, their colors) while remaining themselves. The objects were used partly to describe the persona; partly, however, they were used by the imagination (lodged within the persona) which absorbed them and remolded them into materials for its insight. Here both ways of seeing the relation between self and world are implied. The same ambivalence emerges from his essays, where he turned sharply against the Romantic view that made of imagination a force of life. In "Imagination and Value," he calls the Romantic imagination "minor wish fulfillment" and suggests that it relates to true imagination as sentimentality relates to feeling. He prefers instead to see the imagination as a form of abstraction, a way of getting at the heart of the object.[7] And in "The Noble Rider and the Sound of Words" he relates the vitality of the imagination to the degrees of attachment to reality.[8] All of these statements seem to

6. Cf. Frye, "The Realistic Oriole," *Hudson Review,* X, 355.
7. "Imagination and Value," *A Necessary Angel* (New York, 1951), pp. 138–39.
8. "The Noble Rider and the Sound of Words," *ibid.,* p. 6.

suggest a "realistic" view of the imagination. On the other hand, Stevens also relates the imagination to metaphysics, and sees it as a way of realizing the life of the mind through artifice. A man in Uganda and a man in Paris could share an identical universe of the mind, if it were possible to make such a world palpable by means of artificial creation, that is, through the fictions poetry creates.[9] This view is not unduly different from that of the Romantic imagination, although with a distinctly *fin de siècle* flavor, except that it describes its scope more clearly as an activity of the artistic mind.

The posture created by the idealistic form of the imagination is that of the knower, but one who glances within, who searches in himself for that universalizing mirror which is art. If there is any doubt that critics like Frank Kermode are correct in seeing this romantic strain in Stevens, a glance at Stevens' best-known poems suffices to sustain them. Read "Peter Quince at the Clavier" as a modernized version of "Tintern Abbey" and you will find many parallels. Thus when Wordsworth writes

> These beauteous forms
> Through a long absence have not been to me
> As is a landscape to a blind man's eye

we encounter, negatively, that reflective sight through which the meditative pattern is created, and eyesight is converted into vision. Clearly, there is Peter Quince, the carpenter-clown, bent over the keys of his clavier, whose eye—eliciting through sounds the colors of memory—is turned inward, not blind, but focused on the clash of sense and spirit. The same relationship holds in another famous poem, "Sunday Morning," in which the eye turned inward recreates life and history, and where the meditation proceeds from the eye's feasting on the objects of sense. The more often we read the famous opening lines the more we become aware of their deliberate alternation of sight and vision before the persona is even mentioned:

> Complacencies of the peignoir, and late
> Coffee and oranges in a sunny chair,
> And the green freedom of a cockatoo
> Upon a rug mingle to dissipate
> The holy hush of ancient sacrifice.

R. P. Blackmur told all that needs to be said about these lines more than thirty years ago,[10] yet we might glance at the alternation of

---

9. "Imagination and Value," *ibid.*, p. 140.

10. "Examples of Wallace Stevens," (1931) *Language as Gesture* (New York, 1952), pp. 236-37.

concrete and abstract words he describes from the point of view of the relationship between perceptual and metaphysical awareness. As the lady enjoys sensually the breakfast amenities in the morning sunlight, her very powers of perception begin to draw the aesthetic pattern: the eye focuses on the green cockatoo (somehow linked with freedom) to create a constellation of forms beyond the psyche through which sight is widened into that expanse beyond time which is the poem's subject. This is soon made clear, for when the lady "dreams a little," the objects around her literally merge with a mythical past:

> The pungent oranges among the water-lights
> Seem things in some procession of the dead.[11]

The idealistic form of the imagination, then, depends on the psyche of the poet, or his persona, and ultimately his memory, to produce vision from experience—as Proust used memory to penetrate from sense to vision. Thus each stanza in "Le Monocle de mon Oncle," which plays on the theme of love, is couched in rich perceptual imagery linking present and past. Indeed, the poem's obvious irony lies in the juxtaposition of past ebullience and present vanity in which fruit and bird participate. The blue and the white pigeon, the dark and the rose rabbi of the conclusion lend an ideational meaning to this brilliant juxtaposition: imagination soars. Examples could be multiplied, but none is more poignant than the imaginary voyage of the symbolic hero Crispin in "The Comedian as the Letter C." Here the picaresque traveler's eye is exploited precisely in the Romantic sense, although, of course, with an irony and detachment which was Stevens' own:

> Crispin at sea
> Created, in his day, a touch of doubt.
> An eye most apt in gelatines and jupes,
> Berries of villages, a barber's eye
> An eye of land, of simple salad beds [12]

As the poem progresses, the self undergoes many changes in its search for transcendence, for reality, and for art. A poetic, ironic *Wilhelm Meister* recreated in a modern pattern? If "Peter Quince" is seen as a recomposition of "Tintern Abbey," the "Comedian" may well emerge as a modernized "Prelude" (with the ironic tone of "Don Juan"), describing the growth of a poet's mind and at the same time rendering a poetic. Growth and changes, however, are focused in the *eye* as the intermediary between sense perception and visionary insight.

11. *C.P.*, pp. 66–67.
12. *C.P.*, p. 27.

This romantic function of the eye as a way of achieving self-consciousness and hence imagination, which was recently analyzed in Geoffrey H. Hartman's *Wordsworth's Poetry 1787–1814*, is not the only means of seeing the object. Another stance adopted by Stevens is that of the painter-poet—or perhaps even more aptly, that of the empathizing connoisseur of art—who steps away from the object and yet penetrates to its nature beyond the appearance. This we have called the "realistic" function of the imagination, not in the common sense and literary meaning of mimetic rendition but in the philosophical sense of distinction between subject and object. The poet perceives, but in perceiving mediates between the outward appearance of the object and its essence.

Explicating this aspect of the imagination is simpler in practice than in theory, for Stevens knows what he is about when he faces figures or patterns or paintings, always clearly perceiving a meaning behind the appearances through internal relations within the object or scene. Thus, in the familiar poem, "The Snow Man," the figure dissolves by virtue of its non-sentient (cold) being, seen in relation to a non-sentient landscape, until the true reality, nothingness, remains. Or in the brilliant poem, "Landscape with Boat," the eye's ambivalence between imagination and thing is developed, while the actual figure remains the merest suggestion:

> He brushed away the thunder, then the clouds
> Then the colossal illusion of heaven. Yet still
> The sky was blue. He wanted imperceptible air.
> He wanted to see. He wanted the eye to see
> And not be touched by blue. He wanted to know.[13]

Examples could be multiplied, in which a figure is rendered first, then to be dissolved into its inherent relations (like "The Snow Man"), or in which relations are shown first, then to become a person or a thing (as in "Nude Starting on a Spring Voyage"). Whichever way he took, obviously Stevens had to recreate an atmosphere of the mind, but he was always ambiguous about these matters. In "The Pure Good of Theory" he disdained mere Platonizing. On the one hand, "we see what we think" (as one of his poems is entitled); on the other hand, imagination sees new resemblances in the object which are not reducible to mind. As the well-known poem, "The Glass of Water," indicates, the very changes in the object itself, the states of the substance *water*, can force upon the poet resemblances which may have as much to do with the internal relations in the object as with the

13. *C.P.*, p. 241.

manner of seeing. Our best document for this crucial (and actually fruitful) ambivalence in Stevens is the long poem-poetic, "The Man with the Blue Guitar." In the opening parts of the poem the ambiguity is stated in the form of a dialogue between the audience, wanting to hear things as they are, and the blue guitarist who tells them that his instrument of the imagination cannot make them as they are. But even here the dialogue is not precisely between mimetic realism and imagination. In the very first section, the audience insists on hearing a tune "beyond us, yet ourselves." It wishes to see resemblances beyond experience, yet within the object as it is. But it is the guitarist's despair that he might render only his mind rather than relations among objects. In Section XV he asks:

> Is this picture of Picasso, this "hoard
> Of Destruction" a picture of ourselves?

Ironically he continues:

> Do I sit, deformed, a naked egg.
>
> Catching at Goodbye the harvest moon
> Without seeing the harvest or the moon? [14]

The answer to this ambivalence is partially rendered in "Notes Toward a Supreme Fiction," where the key term is abstraction, that is, that sense of the imagination in which the vision sought by the beholder's eye is also the essence of the thing. The object's meaning, as seen through and beyond the eye, is to be rendered, then to be gathered in a "supreme fiction" of words. Clearly a stable metaphysic and aesthetic are impossible to come by, and we should not make the attempt. Is the "supreme fiction" a third term, as critics often hold, a reconciliation of the object and the perceiving poet? If so, why is it fiction, as Stevens has usually held, unless it assumes that art exists in a predominantly mental climate of its own in which, as he suggested in "Imagination and Value," artifice is created? [15] But all this appears to be contradictory. We can only conclude that change, of being or state, does not lie only in the subject, but in the object as well; that along with philosophy, the reverberations of physics have found their echo in Stevens' poetic epistemology; and that therefore both mind and thing, beholder and scene, self and other, relate to one another in various juxtapositions which are somehow gathered in the language of poetry. But two points remain constant: the poet's eye and the fiction created by the word, the former reflecting the relations between the

14. *C.P.*, p. 173.
15. "Imagination and Value," *A Necessary Angel*, pp. 140–41.

self and the outside world, the latter presenting that fiction in which all relations are rendered. Clearly this is the way *eye* is used in the opening lines of "An Ordinary Evening in New Haven":

> The eye's plain version is a thing apart
> The vulgate of experience. . . .

but which then go on to ask:

> Of what is this house composed if not the sun.

> These houses, these difficult objects, dilapidate
> Appearances of what appearances,

and then concludes:

> A recent imagining of reality
>
> . . . .
>
> A larger poem for a larger audience,[16]

The dual vision of the imagination, then, resolves itself in a single theory of poetry in which selves and objects exist side by side in an identical universe. The hero, the comedian, the tragic knower who is ultimately the poet, perceives a world both outside himself and within. Whatever may have been Stevens' particular theories, he obviously sought both the thing as it is (as one of his late poems declares) and the transfiguring poetic mind. Ideas emerge from the impact of poetry on things and the fictions it constructs as a result of this engagement. The relations he pursues, then, are both realistic and idealistic; they assert, metaphysically, that reality is both mental and physical. Clearly there lies behind this apparent paradox a good deal of nineteenth-century philosophy. As William Burney suggested some years ago in an Iowa doctoral dissertation, despite an affinity for Santayana, Stevens' work shows clear imprints of Hegel's thought. Indeed, Hegelianism expresses precisely the dual vision with which he was so ambiguously concerned. For Hegel viewed as necessary an antagonism of mutually distinct relations which is resolved in an order of the spirit that closely resembles the supreme fiction of Stevens' view, a spirit and an order not reducible to the individual sensibility of the subject, or to the poet's particular mind. But however tempting the analogy, it would resolve neither the questions about the quiddity of the object nor those about the manipulations of the self. Eye and object remain to confront one another and, in their shifting relations, to wrest vision

16. *C.P.*, pp. 465–66.

from sight. If for Stevens their ambivalence is seen through a realistic and idealistic imagination, in Rilke we must look elsewhere.

· 3 ·

"Dasein," wrote Heidegger, "ist nicht ein Vorhandenes . . . , sondern ist primär Möglichkeit." [17] Human existence, unlike that of the empirical world, is not something already present, but primarily a possibility, a forward movement beyond itself. Rilke's work, concerned as it was with the transformation from one state into another of both objects and minds, develops such a projection of being beyond the limits of human nature, while at the same time maintaining the poet's confrontation with the external world. He thus both separates and unifies two modes, being and consciousness, varying them in relation to themselves and to one another. The poet's conversion of sight into vision is maintained, but it points in a different direction.

Rilke's portrayal of perception, like that of identity, was always ambiguous, because it permitted no essential distinction between subject and object. Rilke's view of *Dinge,* which amused Auden, may appear to us as mystical (which it is) and as incredible (which it is not), but it asks us in effect to suspend our disbelief and to see (as does basically every poet) all life as a function of interior experience. Given that premise, Rilke's vision of things as endowed with a presence, or a life, of their own emerges as a natural echo, based on a practicing poet's craft, of the professional philosopher's analysis of the mind. Empathically the poet tries to see behind the questions concerning self and consciousness, and to discern, dramatically and with palpable images, the ambivalences in the nature of objects and selves as they occur in the act of experience.

Unlike Wallace Stevens, whose ambivalence we discerned in two forms of the imagination, Rilke saw the poet's relation to his world as a constant duel with a universe of organic and inorganic nature as alive as himself. Objects act upon the poet's self, which, as Priscilla Washburn Shaw showed admirably in her recent book, *Rilke, Valéry and Yeats: The Domain of the Self,* always had to come to terms with them. Consequently, the poet's self, too, was an object, projecting itself beyond its own nature. The elements, *being* and *consciousness,* are thus contracted within the poet. He is himself—seeing and hearing—

17. *Sein und Zeit* (Halle, 1927), p. 143.

and he is also something else—Angel, Orpheus, Doll, Lament. The confrontation between self and object implicit in cognition is enacted on two different levels and resolves itself in a double action: as things in the physical world impinge upon him, the poet is passive. Objects act upon him, as in Baudelaire's famous poem "Les Bijoux," the alluring, jeweled figure of his mistress first stimulates sense impressions, then evokes a sensual response commanding that very enslavement of the poet by the object of sense which leads to the vision of the infinite, in spiritual death and art. But on the other hand, the poet is also himself, probing the vision, thrusting himself toward the invisible precisely because of his enslavement by the object, since through his union with it in heightened awareness he transforms all outlines of the visible world. The paradox implied in this double gesture is similar to Baudelaire's in the poem we have cited: that of the poet who attains the infinite precisely by being engulfed by the object (whether person, figure, or thing) and by turning it passively into an object of beauty.

An example of this contraction, and its inherent paradox, might be an early sentimental poem about a knight in Rilke's *Book of Pictures*, which juxtaposes the perceiving self, whose vision is directed toward the outside, and its being, its human fate, which exists within. An armored knight rides out into the world seeing "the day and the vale / and the friend and the foe / and the May and the maid / and the wood and Grail," even seeing that "God himself many thousand times / into all the streets has been placed." [18] By contrast, death dwells within, behind the darkest rings of the armor, waiting to be freed from its prison by the "alien" blade. As the knight's eye is turned outward, death's self, his "I," occupies his inward being. In a fascinating reversal, the experiencing self, the knight, is countered by a fate which, speaking through its own voice, thrusts him forward to that unknown but inevitable future when death will be released and the knight will have realized his purpose. This is an obvious inversion of Dürer's famous print, "Knight, Devil, and Death," in which death as well as devil are shown outside, next to the knight in his seemingly invulnerable armor seated on his armored horse as he braves them both in his progress toward a future fate. In Rilke's poem, figures defining the human confrontation of the outside world and those defining his human fate and identity are subtly reversed.

It is, of course, difficult to recognize this strain in Rilke's poetry without accepting the intense inwardness of his vision. On the one

18. *S.W.*, I, 372–73.

hand, his strong commitment to a faithful re-creation of the external world, which critics have often celebrated, is beyond question; but, on the other hand, it always serves a further deeply interior design. As Elizabeth Sewell has shown, the great "Orpheus, Eurydice, Hermes" poem of 1904 renders a picture in which body and mind are deeply intertwined in mine shafts of the underworld that come to us as a strange blend of Novalis' cave and Dante's inferno.[19] In this way, the figures Rilke has created through the media of painting, sculpture, and dramatic monologue always assume a universal structure in which life and death, the visible and invisible, self and objects, are unified—a structure, then, of the poetic imagination whose distances can only be, as with Georges Poulet, "interior distances." Thus the god in "Early Apollo" begins as a shaped rock but is dissolved into perceptions (rose gardens will rise, petals will fall into its open mouth, all things will be present to its sight). Here the anticipation of consciousness tends to dissolve the god's features and thrusts him forward toward human existence.[20]

This sense of an infinite vision arising from a larger structure of the mind, in which the metaphysical awareness compels its object to dissolve into experience, or compels experience to turn into an object, is the great umbrella under which most of Rilke's poetic creation takes place. Another early example, again from the *Book of Pictures*, may clarify this dual relationship. Ostensibly the poem is about fountains, the rising and falling of their water, their Heracleitian fluidity lending the poem its structure. The structure of poem and water, however, is at once seen in the metaphor of objects:

> Auf einmal weiss ich viel von den Fontänen,
> den unbegreiflichen Bäumen aus Glas.

> All at once I know much about fountains
> those unthinkable trees of glass.

Through many metamorphoses, the water passes from the solid trees of glass to tears in the poet's eyes (shed as he was seized by great dreams and then forgotten) to petrified rocks of distant planets and, ultimately, to a recognition of cosmic and human fate. But the manner in which this fate is shown, again a projection of sight, is indicative of Rilke's method. In a surprising inversion, he projects consciousness upon the creatures on the distant stars who try to see us on earth from

19. *The Orphic Voice* (New Haven, Conn., 1960), pp. 327–30.
20. See Ralph Freedman, "Gods, Heroes, and Rilke," *Hereditas: Seven Essays on the Modern Experience of the Classical* (Austin, Tex., 1964).

73

their point of view and imagine us deceptively as secure points of reference. Weeping in their loneliness, those distant creatures may see a reflection of their god upon our faces. The poem concludes:

> (der Gott)
> dessen Bildnis, wie ein Schein aus ihren
> suchenden Lampen, flüchtig und verweht,
> über unsere zerstreuten Gesichter geht.[21]

> (the god)
> whose image—like our searching
> lamp's beam—fleeting, wind-blown,
> passes across our distracted faces.

A god is imagined whose likeness, or *Bildnis*, is at once dissolved into beams of light from searching lamps (instruments of perception), passing vaguely across our distracted faces and thus mirroring his hypothetical presence. The metaphor is the reverse of that of the knight and his internal death, yet achieves a similar end. For the movement of the poem is accomplished because an identical status for consciousness and object, for eye and thing, is assumed with the poem's point of view passing back and forth between them. We begin with water and move to trees of glass, back to eye, and ultimately to petrified stars which are finally reflected inversely upon the perceiving selves. Between these two fields of vision an idea of God is suggested, while the entire image is described by the rising and falling of fountains which embody both activities.

The nature of the rock is described by the epithet *versteint* ("petrified"), while consciousness is suggested by the word *erkennen*. The poem, as we have seen, resolves into a pendulum movement between both these poles. But it is in the final line that the central image for this dual state, here as elsewhere in Rilke, is rendered visible. This image is that of *face* (*Gesicht*), expressing both the activity of seeing and the instrument of sight, the entity through which sight, and perception in general, is expressed. The German word *Gesicht*, of course, literally includes "sight," and the image it creates combines the act of seeing with being seen, that is, the seeing figure. Rilke often uses *Gesicht* in both the active and passive senses. For example, it is beautifully used to describe a gazelle in one of the figures in *New Poems:*

> (Die Gazelle scheint:)
> . . . . hingetragen, als
> wäre mit Sprüngen jeder Lauf geladen
> und schösse nur nicht ab, solang der Hals

21. *S.W.,* I, 456–57.

74

das Haupt im Horchen hält: wie wenn beim Baden
im Wald die Badende sich unterbricht,
den Waldsee im gewendeten Gesicht.[22]

(The gazelle seems:)
· · · · · · · · · · borne along as if
each run (barrel) were loaded with leaps
and were not shot as long as the neck

holds the head in listening: as when, while bathing
in the forest the bather interrupts herself,
the forest lake in her upturned face.

Apart from the magnificently descriptive image of the tension between
head and neck—compared to a shot not fired, the pun of *Lauf* which
can mean "barrel" as well as "run" holding the metaphor together—
the final comparison of the gazelle to the bathing woman suggests how
Rilke develops the term *face* as a reflector and an agent of sensibility.
The tension between the forest lake being seen by and also being
mirrored in the bather's face gives a sense of startled self-consciousness
in the midst of action. It also portrays a reciprocal reflection of lake in
features, of eye in vision, which is symptomatic of *face* as both an
instrument of perception and a manifestation of "being."

This function of *face* as suggesting both existent (thing) and
perceiving is accurately described in one of the sonnets to Orpheus,
which begins as a salute to ancient sarcophagi and then develops the
relationship between life and death, sentience and thinghood, which
are combined in the image of *face*. The sarcophagi are thus at first
compared to the eyes of a newly awakening shepherd, emphasizing the
birth of life—fruit-giving bees sucking their fill, butterflies escaping—
in an inverse relation of life and death familiar from Baudelaire's
"Une Charogne" which Rilke knew well. Singing mouth and seeing
eye supplant the dead objects, as death is turned back into life. But in
Rilke's unified realm, they also project beyond themselves. Song and
silence, life and death, are finally brought together in the single hour
and the human face in which they are concentrated:

Wissen wirs, Freunde, wissen wirs nicht?
Beides bildet die zögernde Stunde
In dem menschlichen Angesicht.[23]

Do we know it, friends, do we not know it?
The hesitant hour forms both
in the human face.

22. *S.W.*, I, 506.
23. *S.W.*, I, 737.

75

The dual purpose of *face* is finally made clear in the important poem "Death of the Poet," where the reciprocal relation between "being" and consciousness is rendered in a sharply dramatic image:

Er lag. Sein aufgestelltes Antlitz war
bleich und verweigernd in den steilen Kissen,
seitdem die Welt und dieses von ihr Wissen
von seinen Sinnen abgerissen,
zurückfiel an das teilnahmslose Jahr.[24]

He lay. His propped-up face was
pale full of refusal in the steep pillows
since the world and all his knowledge of it
had fallen, torn from his senses
(dropped) back into the indifferent year.

The poet's death, the conversion of the living mask into an object, is portrayed in a striking image: the world, and his knowledge, had been torn off his senses, leaving his face (as the poem continues) empty, vulnerable, like an open fruit rotting in the air. Priscilla Washburn Shaw's discussion of this poem, searching as it is, overlooks a crucial point: if the poet's knowing of the world had dropped away after his death, it had once been part of his mask.[25] Through a negative description (their separation after death) we gain a clear indication of the manner in which *face* functions: on the one hand, it is the mask, the persona as well as the organ of perception; on the other hand, it harbors, as in a landscape, the activity of seeing, the act of sight. In this way, Jean Moréas conceived the Symbolist hero: a clown of artifice on whose features sensations and hallucinations are imprinted to compound a mask of tragic, suffering humanity.

Rilke's use of *face* or *Gesicht* is, of course, merely symptomatic of his general manner of projecting self and thing as manifestations of "being," and at the same time rendering their interrelation in the act of knowledge. For it illustrates Rilke's general tendency to see objects (space) in terms of activity (time) and activity in terms of objects. This reciprocal projection is not only responsible for Rilke's technique of animation but also, precisely as it underlines his ambivalence, for his vision of the unity of life and death, the visible and the invisible.

24. *S.W.*, I, 495–96.
25. Priscilla Washburn Shaw, *Rilke, Valéry and Yeats: The Domain of the Self* (New Brunswick, N. J., 1964), pp. 12–13. Mrs. Shaw here refers to the function of the physical as well as perceptual and spiritual dimensions of *Gesicht*, which she sees as one of the manifestations of Rilke's concept of self.

The large poem "Hetärengräber," for example, which describes the remains of sensuous beings through things, including the things their own bodies have become (their teeth compared to chess sets), returns in the end to the shifting surface of a river under which the bodies lie embedded. Such a dissolution of objects first defined by sensuality into a new sensuous life (water) is another example of the way in which things are transformed into their counterpoints. Especially in *New Poems,* we find many representations of figures whose meaning is understood through an activity—acting or perceiving or being transformed or dissolved.

Images like face, water, or mirror—conventional Symbolist images indeed—are the means whereby, in a new way, the transition from empirical to metaphysical perception is accomplished. The manner is new, because, unlike even the most stringent of Symbolists, Rilke draws no line between the two types of experience. Mallarmé renders objects as ideal conversions of themselves, in which the self is a prophet or Hérodiade, the lonely self-enclosed virgin whose gardens are *jardins d'améthyste.* It is the converse of naturalism, which uses objects to displace the spirit. But for Rilke both realms are fused. Hence, the reciprocity of his perception. Not only are matter and mind interchangeable; subject and object are interchangeable as well. For they are mutually distinct and reversible so that each may assume the role of the other. Hence, if we encounter a fresh metaphysical perception in Rilke's art, it is of a very different kind.

Rilke's type of perception, which combines both terms of the relation implicit in knowledge (subject and object) and yet relates them to one another as if they were mutually exclusive, is embodied in both the figure and the role of the Angel of the *Duino Elegies.* For the Angel, as described, for example, in "The Second Duino Elegy," is endowed with all the characteristics we have analyzed in our discussion of Rilke's imagination: the ambivalence between subject and object and the tendency to dissolve perception and being into one another. The Angel is defined by an accumulation of all things which form part of himself, but also of all possible experience, including, as in "Death of the Poet," all landscapes, all things whether made by men or created by God.

> Frühe Geglückte, ihr Verwöhnten der Schöpfung,
> Höhenzüge, morgendliche Grate
> aller Erschaffung—Pollen der blühenden Gottheit,
> Gelenke des Lichtes, Gänge, Treppen, Throne,
> Räume aus Wesen, Schilde aus Wonne, Tumulte

stürmisch entzückten Gefühls und plötzlich, einzeln,
Spiegel: die die entströmte eigene Schönheit
wiederschöpften zurück in das eigene Antlitz.[26]

In Leishman and Spender's translation:

Early successes, Creation's pampered darlings,
ranges, summits, dawn-red ridges
of all beginning, pollen of blossoming godhead,
hinges of light, corridors, stairways, thrones,
spaces of being, shields of felicity, tumults
of stormily rapturous feeling and suddenly, separate,
mirrors, drawing up their own
outstreamed beauty into their faces again.[27]

In this projected figure of the Angel, the unity of being and consciousness is envisaged in perfect harmony. The possibility of human existence, in Heidegger's sense, is thrust outward beyond man towards God's perfect creation. Moreover, by gazing into the mirror where his perfection is reproduced, the Angel defines himself through an act of perceiving which is in itself complete. At the same time, by drawing his beauty onto himself, the Angel projects it upon the mirror and returns it whole, describing Rilke's version of the interchange of eyesight and vision. Unlike Stevens, in whom we noted idealistic and realistic conceptions of the imagination side by side, Rilke acts upon an awareness of his own ambivalence between being and perceiving and personifies its perfect resolution (unattainable for human beings) in the figure of the Angel, or, later on, in that of Orpheus. In a curiously complex relationship, in which sight and vision interact, the Angel becomes a collective consciousness including both being and perceiving, metaphysical and empirical knowledge.

· 4 ·

We have examined two attitudes—two versions of a poetic in the verse of two modern poets who spoke literally from two different points in the Western world. They engaged in no dialogue, but rather spoke like two soliloquists at different ends of the same stage, addressing an identical audience and clarifying to themselves the essential tasks faced by the poet of their time. Their poetic derived from similar presuppositions and a similar uncertainty. The presuppo-

---

26. *S.W.*, I, 689.
27. *Duino Elegies*, trans. Leishman and Spender (New York, 1939), p. 29.

sitions rested on the poet's condition as he emerged from the intellectual experimentations which we now view broadly as the Symbolist experience. It consisted of an intense awareness of the relation between the self and a world which is always other than itself, a world in which appearances seen and appraised by the artist's eye are mere suggestions for a further reality. At the same time, a modern consciousness views this endeavor as part of our compulsive need to clarify, explain, and analyze, through poetry, the mechanisms by which our knowledge is obtained and the standards by which it is justified.

This very endeavor, unconsciously perhaps, created the uncertainty of Rilke's and Stevens' views about the relationship between poetry and the world it explores, which, in turn, became the center of the aesthetic they shared. For Stevens, imagination was a central term, a term that naturally emerged from the Emersonian tradition, varied by the total idealism of Mallarmé. It was not, however, wholly reducible to philosophical analogies, or other poetic theories, for they were all resisted by the stubborn verse itself which constantly reflected two types of experience: that in which selves developed poetic analogies from within the object, keeping the separation of poet and world intact, and that in which both are united in a superior realm through which impersonal ideas and forms are apprehended. Rilke, who had learned not only from Cézanne and Rodin but from Nietzsche as well, saw this ambivalence in terms both larger and narrower: the poet reflects an image of human existence, reconciling all dichotomies in the visible and invisible world, as well as a concern with the conditions of experience in the artist's mind as he engages the objects around him. Things had to be resolved into states of mind, as states of mind ultimately reverted to things or states of being. This ambivalence is more obvious in Rilke and Stevens than in many other modern poets, as, for example, in Eliot or Yeats, who seemed to project more definite points of reference—mystical, theological, or historical—in terms of which relations between selves and objects could be seen. For the two poets we have examined, the system was defined by the "given" of experience itself as well as by the compulsion to analyze and represent our knowledge of that which is and that which is not, of finite and infinite experience.

The issue faced by the two poets, their ambivalence between a realistic and idealistic imagination, between consciousness and being, can be resolved only if both elements are viewed in an identical structure of the mind. Kant's critiques charted this structure, endeavoring to include in their analysis not only the representation of things to minds by which we chart our course, but also the realm behind the world of sense which became so peculiar a domain for poets. If Kant stopped short of extending the possibility of rational knowledge to this transcendental realm as well, and left this assertion to his successors, he nonetheless created the structure through which an empirical confrontation with objects might press on to metaphysical knowledge. It is in this sense that the images of *eye* and *face*, which we examined in Stevens and Rilke, obtain their general meaning, for each conveys a special relation between experience and meta-experience, between perception and being, within the total realm of the mind.

Eye and sight, face and vision, thus become the terms by which a special phase in modern poetics can be defined. It is a continuation of Coleridge's imagination: the eye's apprehension of the unknowable, the transcendent vision. The Ancient Mariner's glittering eye holding the wedding-guest's transfixed; the wedding guest's eye being held by the mariner's gaze—these are the parallels to the kind of imagination we have traced. In the poems of Wallace Stevens and Rainer Maria Rilke, then, we face neither Dante's dramatization of hell and paradise, nor Donne's contractions of sense and thought, but an analysis, in the spirit of Coleridge, which dissects and recreates the metaphysical leap from sensing to knowing the unknowable within a continuing posture of cognition.

The Inward Muse

DONALD HALL

I AM ASKED to talk about the critic *in* the poet, or the function of the critical intelligence in the creative process. Therefore I must give an account of the creative process as a whole. Since no one has ever defined the creative process convincingly, I have a lot to accomplish in a short space.

To investigate the process of writing poems, one can go to a number of sources for ideas and information; one can go to literary history and learn about the habits and manuscripts of great authors. One can go to literary theory and discover the illogic of some of our presuppositions. One can go to the huge literature about creativity which is emerging from psychology, especially psychoanalytical psychology. (Most of my reading in the last few months has been in this third area, and I will try to make use—in an eclectic and unscientific way—of what I have learned.) But I suspect that a fourth source has determined my choices among the data supplied by the other three, and has picked what fits and ignored what doesn't fit; the fourth source is introspection, memory, scrutiny of my own experience of making poems.

Even to talk about the critical intelligence in the creative process is to suggest a possible mistake, because it implies a separation between two types of thinking which is rarely discernible in practice. Almost all writing about the creative process, whether by poets or critics or psychoanalysts, has involved a theoretical dualism of *creation* which provides material, and *criticism* which shapes it. When Eliot wrote that "The critical activity finds its highest, truest fulfillment in *a kind of union* with creation in the labour of the artist" (my italics), he was writing the epigraph for my contribution to the subject of "the poet as critic." More typical is Edmund Bergler's separation of the process into two *phases*, as if they occurred in sequence. The first phase is the release of material from the id, distorted indeed—a system of drives, defenses, and counterdefenses. Then, "The second phase consists of work, often hard work, to form and develop the material received from unconscious sources; experience, tact, great technical skill are needed in this phase." How neat and orderly we are. Buried in this scheme is an economic metaphor of raw material, factory and consumer. Dr. Bergler ignores the psychological meaning of "technical skill"—a cliché as he uses it—and concentrates only on drives and defenses. He also displays an unacknowledged puritanism: after the orgy of the id, there is the hard work of the consciousness. This dualism conjures up fantastic scenes: from a dim swamp there emerges the hulking green monster of the id, its jaws drooling blood as it looks for another child to eat; then, separate, appears the critical intelligence, cheerful, walking in the bright sun, wearing sensible shoes, a clean little lady with an umbrella. When she encounters the monster she *works hard* on him, reforms him, and—presto!—he becomes John V. Lindsay, both disciplined and handsome.

The responsibility for many of the misleading ideas about the creative process belongs to poets. Poets tend to represent themselves either as detached craftsmen or as inspired, unconscious, mad mouthpieces. Poe is the ultimate craftsman, at least in his pose. One may not accept that the outside—the pose—represents what really happens inside, but poses are serious; as Pasternak said, you need the pose before you can have the poem. Poe tells us that he planned "The Raven" formally before he thought of the content, that he arrived at the subject, the death of a beautiful woman, rationally; perhaps indeed this was the way it seemed to him. In another context, T. S. Eliot wrote, "One might even hazard the conjecture that the care for perfection of form, among some of the romantic poets of the nineteenth century, was an effort to support, or to conceal from view, an inner disorder." Poe *had* to write necrophilia; therefore in order to write at all his consciousness had to deny his obsession. He could only write "The Raven" if he treated it like a crossword puzzle. Oscar Wilde has Gilbert say, in *The Critic as Artist,* "All fine imaginative work is self-conscious and deliberate. No poet sings because he must sing." Here we must understand that the author of *The Picture of Dorian Gray* is concealing from himself the emotional necessity of his work.

The pose of being detached from the content, or of being interested only in technique, is what allows the forbidden content to happen. I remember talking to W. D. Snodgrass once about some new techniques that each of us were trying out—something utterly complicated and probably, from the point of view of the reader, pointless—like a syllabic stanza of eighty-seven syllables in which every thirteenth word began with *w*. And Mr. Snodgrass said that the reason we concentrate so much on technique is that this absorption of the consciousness may allow a previously censored content to seep up onto the page. With awareness of psychoanalytical theory, one becomes conscious of the possibilities of stimulating parts of one's psyche. The technique of removing or absorbing the surface of the mind is an old one. Gertrude Stein used to write in a car parked at a Paris intersection—all those horns beeping, and Hart Crane on occasion wrote drinking wine and playing Ravel's "Bolero" over and over again. Northrop Frye says somewhere that "It takes a great deal of will-power to write poetry, but some of the will must be used to relax the will." Here the use of the same word for two things helps to relieve us of the fallacy of a division between critical and creative.

Some poets use technique to absorb the will; others use alcohol to relax it. Really—though they look utterly different—they are doing the same thing. They are outmaneuvering the restrictiveness and timidity of the conscious mind. I am proposing a unitary view of the creative process. I wish to suggest that the poets who give divergent accounts of their own processes are *using* their accounts in order to move toward a center. Even the convention among Greek poets of being mad, as Plato reports it, was a pose that could stimulate the removal of conscious barriers. I do not believe that Blake really hallucinated voices; those voices came back and dictated revisions. For that matter, I don't believe that "Kubla Khan" was a dream-poem. I think one must be skeptical of all extreme accounts of process. Whenever I hear a poet talking manic possession, I hear a man possessed by a self-protective consciousness, who is looking for a way out.

A poem happens when different aspects of the mind manage to *coincide*. Keats said, "My judgement is as active when I am writing as my imagination." There they are again, under different names, the two sides. But judgment and imagination coincided in the same actions, made "a kind of union." To write (or to cross out) a word was simultaneously an act of judgment and of imagination, of the critic and of the creator. There are, of course, different moments in the process of writing a poem. Often a poem will start with wild excitement and finish some months later with slow consideration. There is the story of Shelley observed scribbling a poem in haste, and then telling his observer, "In the morning, when cooled down, out of the rude sketch . . . I shall attempt a drawing." The drawing is as imaginative and as creative as the sketch; new words must be found, new decisions made; imagination and judgment must continue to coincide. Often in the long process of writing a poem there will be a second or a third moment of wild excitement followed by slow consideration.

One of the fascinating phenomena in dealing with a mental event is the way in which the same technique can be used for opposite purposes. Take rhyme for example. A conventional defense of rhyme —I remember Howard Nemerov speaking of it somewhere—is that it gives the poet ideas, stimulates his imagination, by suggesting (through the search for new sounds) words, ideas, symbols, and metaphors which would otherwise not have occurred to him. Rhyme is a kind of creative accident, more controlled than paint-splashing, but largely fortuitous. On the other hand, Dryden praised rhyme for a reason that must seem almost opposite; he preferred rhyme to blank verse because it *curbed* his fancy, held him down, kept him from going on and on. Really, both statements could be made by the same poet. But the fact that one poet emphasizes rhyme as an opener-up, and another, rhyme as a closer-down, reveals that each poet is seeking to complete himself; each poet is searching for the unification of imagination and choice.

Bad poetry is a result of defective creative process, which is a result of neurosis (the inability to unify the psychic components of creativity may be caused by anxiety over regression, for instance). Sometimes there is a discernible imbalance in the just-bad poem, but since poetry is a unity, an imbalance usually causes everything to be wrong. Any poetry editor will tell you that most of what he sees is unrevised garbage, slewed out verses in which there is no attempt at significant order. Yet, if one said that it was merely lacking in technical skill, one would imply that there was an appreciable content to which there was applied insufficient talent or technical experience. This is aesthetically invalid, psychologically invalid—and invisible in the text. One doesn't discern great emotions undisciplined by form—horses without reins—because such things are not discernible in poetry. A mute inglorious "Lycidas" is as unlikely as a mute inglorious Milton. Likewise, the contrary fault, which fills the literary magazines, is not small emotions overcontrolled. That's impossible too. A tiny subject, or not very moving poem, can be boring perhaps, but it's more likely to be satisfying if the form is precise, finished, whole. What we abhor is the poem in which the language and form have the rhetoric, the roll and sweep of great emotions, which are not made actual or present in the poem. This is the case of the reins without the horse, or more accurately, the reins faking the horse.

The creative process is at fault when a poem fails—but that's tautology, because you can tell the process fails only when the poem fails. But we have asserted healthy creative process as the simultaneity of complementary qualities in the act of writing. It is time to become more empirical and to observe as much as possible of this process in which judgment and imagination are one. Frank Barron speaks of "an incessant dialectic between integration and diffusion," and Marion Milner talks of an oscillation between the "oceanic state" (in *Civilization and its Discontents,* Freud described the oceanic feeling: that diffuse sense of belonging to all and being sensitive to all, which Freud relates to the baby's sense of oneness with the breast and indeed the rest of the universe) and the surface mind. Now I don't believe that it is the surface mind which is usually in question, as I will make clear in a moment, but I do think that there *is* an oscillation so rapid as hardly to seem to occupy time, between a diffuse attentive expectancy, into which words or phrases float, and another observing part of the mind which takes note and measures. I do not mean simply to give new names to the old creative-critical split, however. The two ends of the oscillation both include imagining and judging. The depth mind to which we pay diffused attention does not simply supply unjudged, undifferentiated material. Although I believe, for whatever it means, that a regression is involved, and that the depth mind even as we are able to glimpse it shows characteristics of the primary process like condensation and identification, the fact remains that changes and choices occur—critical actions—before the conscious intellect appears or knows what is going on at all. (I am assuming that I can call *critical* whatever discriminates, judges, and chooses—whether or not it is conscious.)

Poems begin any number of ways, but here is a frequent way. It is snowing, the first snow of the year. I become sleepy with the snow, I relax, daydream, enter that sleepy and almost hallucinating state I recognize as preluding a poem; my spirit wanders out of myself into the snow, and phrases come into my head. Suddenly I realize that snow does this to me, every year, especially first snow. I must write about it in order to try to understand it. Snow is, in psychoanalytic language, overdetermined for me. It is burdened with affect, heavy with a nameless emotion. Being overdetermined, it must have multiple sources. I try to keep my attention diffuse and responsive to suggestion, my pen moving, as one thing leads to another down the page. I am trying to reach, be true to, exploit, the multiple sources of this overdetermination,

I don't take dictation from my unconscious mind. As I write, there is no question of simply putting down what I think. I think too fast, too much, to write down all of it, or even to dictate it if I had a machine by me. (It is for this reason that we cannot take seriously the policy of nonrevision, advocated by so serious a man as Robert Duncan on the assumption that the revision is false to the original form of the poem in the mind; this policy implies that the poem was, at one time, a single thing and not a horde of alternatives.) Words come into my head, flipping over like a deck of cards. Sometimes I choose, pausing a moment and having reasons; most of the time the word written down is one that presents itself saying pretty please, bowing. You know those series of choices that poets always put in the margins of their worksheets: large, small, tiny, huge, green, horrid, aimless, yellow. One of them—say "yellow"—comes into the mind wearing italics. It is overdetermined; it announces itself as already chosen. The multiple sources may include the image of the color, the associations with certain flowers, the oral pleasure of the syllables in the context, and a hundred other things—one is seldom aware of them at the time.

In a later draft, the word "yellow" may one day find itself discarded. One trusts the affect at the start, and writes the word down, knowing that the conviction of its rightness may prove to be perfectly incorrect. (The worst poems in the world have been written down with a certainty of inspired genius. So have the best.) The word which seemed so right at the start may turn out wrong because the poem changed as it developed; a poem as it grows sets its own standard, by which each component of the poem will have to be judged. Or more likely, the cathexis involved only a part of the word. One made a judgment (the word seemed to come forth already judged) forgetting something—that "yellow" in a poem about snow reminds one of dogs urinating perhaps, or that a near-rhyme with "hero" is jarring to the ear. But my point is that some form of judgment or criticism is involved in the writing down of any word, good or bad, in any draft.

There is also the shape of the poem on the page and to the ear. This takes us to the second half of our oscillating pair. There is in the mind of the poet a great deal of learned form, technique, and mastery, of which he is not immediately conscious. The preconscious has been invented to take care of this sort of thing. This formal activity takes place, I think, neither in the depth mind, with its drives and defenses and counterdefenses, nor on the surface mind (*contra* Marion Milner), with its reasons and its secondary elaboration. The depth mind has no sense of a gestalt, which is perhaps one reason why babies aren't great writers. The preconscious is the primary locus of the satisfaction one feels in the *wholeness* of a work of art.

One of my old teachers, when he urges his students to acquire poetic techniques, likes to talk about the training of Joe Louis who apparently began life as a prize fighter lacking in footwork. His trainers marked the gym floor with chalk to set him exercises, over and over—rather like doing heroic couplets with medial caesuras—until he had the moves by heart and did them without thinking. There *is* thinking in writing poetry (I suspect there is in prize fighting), but an enormous amount of our judging, deciding, choosing is made without conscious thought. A sense of poetic form becomes "second nature," as the idiom has it. The satisfaction we feel in the achieved gestalt is the click of the lid of the perfectly made box, which Yeats heard in the finished poem.

The preconscious of a poet comes from all the poems he has read, the criticism he has read, the language he has used and heard used, and the arguments he has had with his friends. It works, as the poem unfolds itself down the page, as a system of possibilities, like the system of the sonnet, or the system of blank verse, but infinitely more various than those superficial forms. I do think that knowledge of sonnet form and blank verse does reside in the preconscious. Anyone who has had much experience of either form has acquired a great deal of knowledge which will inform his choices without being verbalized. But in free verse as well, our preconscious has acquired, through reading and talking and thinking, ideas of what a good noise may sound like. Maybe the word "yellow" was chosen instead of the word "gold" because the cadence rejected a monosyllable at this point in the poem. If so, the preconscious was imagining and judging poetic form. "Ear"

DONALD HALL

—that mysterious word which poets love—is a quality of the preconscious mainly, I think. Articulated ear, the movement of the whole
poem in time, is surely preconscious. There is the other kind of ear—
Dylan Thomas as opposed to Milton—which is unimpressive as a long
rhythm but satisfying in the immediate pronunciation. This second
kind of ear is an oral satisfaction while the longer rhythmic type is a
gestalt satisfaction. Oral satisfaction, to some degree, is present in all
good poems, and comes I think more from unconscious, instinctual
sources—a regression to the pleasure of the infant at the breast—than
from conscious or preconscious formal standards, which pertain to the
ego.

In writing the poem about snow, the words seemed naturally to fall
into six-line, free-verse stanzas, two or three accents a line. Six months
later, I suspect, the form would have been different. Sometimes one
chooses a type of line on purpose, but most often in my experience a
poem seems to choose its own. However, if I think hard enough, I can
usually figure out the circumstances which led to the particular line
and stanza. The choice was not conscious, but it is explicable. For
instance, one day I find myself thinking something like this: "I've been
writing all my free verse in lines of about the same length and in
stanzas; that's because I have a nostalgia for tight rhymed iambic
forms; why not be brave and go in for asymmetry all the way?" Two
weeks later when a poem starts to come, it presents itself as asymmet-
rical, though I do not will it to come so. The preconscious has
absorbed my earlier conscious thought and erected it into a temporary
and tentative standard.

I have been using two different ideas—unconscious overdetermination and preconscious knowledge—to talk about critical choices made
when one is not being conscious. Let me talk about one more poem. In
the snow poem, I was trying to understand my overresponse to a
natural phenomenon. A month or two after writing about the snow, a
phrase came into my head, unattached to anything natural—I have
never discovered the source of it, in my reading or in conversation—
simply the name of an animal, the musk-ox. And with it came a
rhythm, a highly percussive and strange beat. I had no idea what it
meant, but it came bearing the credentials of strong feeling and I
trusted it as I have learned to do. I worked out the rhythm consciously,
and over two years hammered out a short poem which has virtually no
rational content. (It is a short inconsequential narrative.) By the end
of the two years I began to see what, in a sense, I was talking about. To
my surprise at least a few other people understood it too. In this poem
the working out of the rhythm (a scheme of louds and softs irregularly

88

spaced from line to line, but each stanza repeating the same line-structure) gave me great trouble, absorbed consciousness, allowed me to think of the poem as music or abstract painting, and so allowed the poem to explore an area of sexual feeling which I would otherwise have kept hidden from myself. In this case a consciousness of form—in the obvious sense of repeated measure—absorbed consciousness. Of course at the same time, all my years of reading and technical striving were at work preconsciously, measuring and judging the poise of syllables, the rub of a verb against a noun, the degree of an enjambment.

Most of the deciding and the criticizing, then, takes place as the hand moves; and the hand moves before the consciousness tells it to move. (There is a final nit-picking stage at which I interrogate the poem consciously, but it generally contributes little to the poem as a whole.) There is no kind of balance between conscious and unconscious in a poem, because their is so little that is fully conscious. But there is an oscillation, and even within the extremes of the oscillation —where directions from unconscious sources are deployed under the conditions of preconsciousness—there is a certain doubleness in the psyche of the poet, and in the definition of the poem.

The definition of a good poem, I have always said, requires the idea of an audience. That audience can be one person—probably *is* one person—but it is someone other than the poet. The poet, if he is a good one, has to include this critic in his own psyche. It is part of the psychic machinery that makes a poet. The Muse, I strongly suspect, is the critic-God within us, to whom all poems are truly addressed. A few years back, answering a question about the audience at which a poem is aimed, Richard Wilbur named the Muse, and said the Muse was invented to cover up the fact that the poem was addressed to nobody in particular. I agree that the Muse is the reader, but not that she is no one in particular. Superficially she is a compound of our six best friends, our wife, and Shakespeare; really, she is probably good old Mom. She is another survival of infancy, like most of the things that make a poem. When a baby has the oceanic feeling and then is deprived of his contact with the breast, he invents (believes in) an eaten-up mother, who by his fantasy lives inside him. He takes the outside world into himself, and becomes an autarchy, subject and object, creator and appreciator, eventually poet and critic. The oscillation in the creative process, so rapid as to be invisible, is between the mother giving milk (poet giving out words) and the baby drinking it (critic exercising his taste). I am aware that I have just had the critic as both mother and baby, the poet as both baby and mother; reversibility is a characteristic of the depth mind. There are pregnancy fantasies involved here too. A book is a birth, and who has not experienced that postpartum depression?

Inside this small world of the creative process, peopled by the giver and the receiver, a dialogue continues as the poem changes and becomes more and more solid or objectified or firm in its formulation. Then the dialogue moves outside or closer to outside, although always, I think, on the model of the autarchy and with reference to the autarchy. When my poems are new I cannot show them to anyone at all. The psychic balance, the necessary oscillation, would be interrupted by the presence of an exterior spirit. Three's a crowd. Later comes a moment when I seek out the opinion of friends, by letter or in person; at first only a few, then when the poem is more secure, a greater number. But there is really an intermediate step, a dialogue not with the faceless Muse that I have eaten, but with imagined friends. I don't do it on purpose, though I could, I think. It is a way of testing the poem, objectifying it a bit further. I think: What will Robert think of this? Louis? Their voices speak to me, in characteristic accents and language. Sometimes I get angry with them for their obtuseness or nastiness; at other times suddenly they say something negative and acute, that I hadn't known about the poem. My fantasy of another voice, another way of thinking, has shown me something I didn't know. The hand without being bidden crosses out a line.

I must admit that when I was younger I invented the voices of well-known elders who criticized me. Though I daydreamed sometimes of applause from Mr. Eliot and Mr. Pound—"Well done, Hall!" "By God, you've done it again!"—these daydreams were only like the eternal cables from Sweden inviting me to accept the Nobel Prize. It was not they who gave me criticism, but an editor and critic and poet who was nearly a literary dictator for a brief period, although I doubt that he aspired to such status. I grew up in the thick of the new criticism, and as I stared at my young verses I could sometimes hear the voice of Mr. Ransom, whom I had never met, intimating, "Mistuh Hall, you ah pleased to be ironical?" It took me ten years to get rid of that voice. And I have tried not merely to substitute the voice of Theodore Roethke or Charles Olson; and I cannot really enclose the Chilean voice of Pablo Neruda.

Objectifying is a series of concentric circles. First there is the oscillation between breast and baby. Then there is the imagined dialogue and the real dialogue with friends. For me, there is also a point at which it is useful to read the poem aloud at a poetry reading. One is not after comments from the crowd, but a speechless feedback.

Really, it is simply an aid to the eaten-up Muse that lives inside us. (This is what I mean when I say that all objectification occurs in relation to the autarchy.) The faces listening make the poem more distant, frame it, print it. I have at times instantly seen a flaw in a poem the first time I read it to an audience. At another level of objectivity there is magazine publication. Frequently, when I compare a Robert Lowell poem, in magazine and book, I find he has revised and improved it. Then there is book publication. One reason some poets lust after selection and collection is not so much vanity as a desire to improve their poems, to alter the record.

The poet is a critic wherever he sits down to write, because he has a critic inside him. The critic—like any critic worth his salt—knows what he likes before he knows why he likes it. The critic is two things in particular: the one I have called a critic is not the usual one; he is the choice by overdetermination from the depth mind. The other is almost a traditional critic; the creation of a set of standards, changing, enlarging, narrowing as the poet ages and reads and endures, existing first of all in the preconscious but reachable by the intelligence, particularly through the use of the psychic device of internal dialogue, in the oscillation of kinds of vision. Mostly, one knows as one grows older to trust the inward Muse, to try to adjust one's psyche so that the dialogue between the parts of one's autarchy is not interrupted. We search for a receptive passivity, thinking of the poem as a creature within us, within the unimaginable complex which *is* us, but over which our consciousness has small control. Let me end my essay by quoting a small poem that I wrote several years ago, which is appropriate, I think, to these reflections. It is called:

THE POEM
It discovers by night
what the day hid from it.
Sometimes it turns itself
into an animal.
In summer it takes long walks
by itself where meadows
fold back from ditches.
Once it stood still
in a quiet row of machines.
Who knows
what it is thinking?

The Poet as Critic,
the Critic as Poet,
the Poet-Critic

RENÉ WELLEK

6

I AM TODAY out of order or out of place. At the canonization of a saint, I know, the Devil's advocate, *advocatus diaboli,* has to be heard first, while I come at the end of a program devoted to the beatification or even sanctification of the poet-critic. Still, I should like, at least, to ask a few questions and to throw some doubts on the possibility and desirability of the union between poet and critic.

We might ask whether the poet *qua* poet can be a critic? Can he be, or has he been, in history, a good critic? Has his being a critic been good for criticism? Or to reverse the direction of our questioning: has criticism been good for the poet? Has the union of the poet-critic or critic-poet been successful? Has he been a "house divided against himself" or has he been or can he be the integrated man of both sensibility and intellect?

T. S. Eliot in his "Brief Treatise on the Criticism of Poetry" [1] distinguishes three types of criticism: the first is the so-called "creative criticism" which is really "etiolated creation," of which Pater serves as a horrible example. (Incidentally this is quite unjust, as Pater, with the exception of the notorious Mona Lisa passage, hardly ever wrote such "creative criticism." [2]) The second type, historical and moralistic criticism, is represented by Sainte-Beuve. The third type, criticism proper, the only genuine criticism, is that of the poet-critic who is "criticising poetry in order to create poetry." [3] Eliot forgets or ignores the philosophers and theorists who actually determined the history of criticism and who were neither frustrated poets nor historians nor moralists nor poets, although Eliot allows on occasion a single exception, Aristotle.[4] But his success, which was surely greater than that of any other critic in the history of criticism, is quite inexplicable in Eliot's scheme.

Eliot at a later period recognized the limitations of the poet as critic; the poet, he then acknowledged, always tries "to defend the kind of poetry he is writing." [5] In a lecture, "To Criticize the Critic," given at Yale (and elsewhere at about the same time) in November, 1961, and recently published for the first time, he disparaged his own criticism as a mere by-product of his creative activity, as written strictly within the context of the literature of the time. Eliot professes irritation with having his "words, perhaps written thirty or forty years ago, quoted as if I had uttered them yesterday." His criticism is not a "design for a massive critical structure." He is puzzled by the vogue of such terms as "dissociation of sensibility" or "objective correlative." He is always at a loss for what to say when "earnest scholars, or schoolchildren, write to ask [him] for an explanation." [6] Eliot's so-called recantation of his criticism of Milton appeals expressly to the practical situation. In 1936 Milton would have been a bad influence on the writing of poetry; in 1947 we are allowed to admire him, as his example has ceased to be dangerous to young poets.[7] Eliot consistently

1. *Chapbook*, No. 2 (1920).
2. See the chapter on Pater in my *History of Modern Criticism* (New Haven, Conn., 1965), IV, 382 ff.
3. "The Perfect Critic," *The Sacred Wood* (London, 1920), p. 14.
4. *Ibid.*, pp. 9–10.
5. "The Music of Poetry," *On Poetry and Poets* (London, 1957), p. 26.
6. *To Criticize the Critic* (London, 1965), pp. 14, 19.
7. See *On Poetry and Poets*, pp. 138 ff.

judges his criticism as strictly occasional, written for his own use and that of other poets; and he hardly ever recognizes that criticism has been written mainly for other people than poets.

Similarly, W. H. Auden admits that the critical opinions of a writer "are for the most part, manifestations of his debate with himself as to what he should do next and what he should avoid." The poet is "a critic who is only interested in one author and only concerned with works that do not yet exist." Auden even says "in unkind moments one is almost tempted to think that all [the poets] are really saying is: 'Read me! Don't read the other fellows!' " "The poet's judgments as he reads are of this kind: 'My God! My Great-Grandfather! My Uncle! My Enemy! My Brother! My imbecile Brother!' " [8]

It would be easy to buttress this recognition of the inevitable egocentricity and narrowness of a poet's criticism by examples drawn from history. To limit myself to the criticism of great English poets, think how Dryden advocates blank verse or rhyme with contradictory arguments at different moments of his career as a dramatist; or think how unjust Wordsworth was to poets like Thomas Gray or Keats who did not conform to his theory of plain diction. Think how mistaken Coleridge was in preferring Schiller to Goethe, or how capricious Yeats's selections in the introduction to *The Oxford Book of Modern Verse* appear even to the most sympathetic reader. But we should reflect that non-poets as critics have committed as many and as egregious critical errors as poets, and that non-poet critics are just as inevitably provided with their own sets of blinkers—ideological or aesthetic or just personal—which might narrow their vision even more drastically.

We must come, however, to the conclusion that a poet is creating a concrete work of art and that he does not necessarily either know or care about the nature of his activity and certainly may not be able to formulate it in intellectual terms. Moreover, the poet is not necessarily able to fulfil the critic's main judicial function: the evaluation of the poetry of other poets. Oscar Wilde put this lesson in his witty way: "Indeed, so far from its being that the artist is the best judge of art, a really great artist can never judge of other people's work at all, and can hardly, in fact, judge of his own. That very concentration of vision which makes a man an artist, limits by its sheer intensity his faculty of fine appreciation. . . . Creation employs all its critical faculty within its own sphere. It may not use it in the sphere that belongs to others. It

8. *The Dyer's Hand and Other Essays* (New York, 1962), pp. 5, 9–10, 33, 52.

is exactly because a man cannot do a thing that he is the proper judge of it." [9]

Still, we cannot be satisfied with this conclusion. Oscar Wilde himself was not and did actually recommend "creative criticism," criticism as a work of art, the invasion of criticism by poetry. Criticism, he argued, is itself an art. It treats the work of art simply as a starting point for new creation, as a suggestion for new work of the critic's own that need not necessarily bear any obvious resemblance to the thing he criticizes. Wilde here accepts Anatole France's famous proposal that the critic record "the adventures of his soul among masterpieces," that he speak of himself "on the occasion of Shakespeare or Racine, Pascal or Goethe." [10] Self-expression, even autobiography, is the aim, which, at least in the theoretical formulations, would be entirely divorced from the object "as it really is," and thus criticism, we may conclude, need not be concerned with works of art, but could have its starting point in almost everything under the sun. If we are concerned with criticism as organized knowledge, as interpretation and judgment of publicly verifiable objects, we must dismiss poetic criticism as an irrelevancy. To-day the Mona Lisa passage in Pater, the ostentatious fireworks of Swinburne's eloquence, and even the charming reflections of Anatole France have lost their appeal and are no present danger.

But fictional criticism is by no means a thing of the past. It is with us in a new guise: that of the myth critic like Northrop Frye, who spins his fancies in total disregard of the text and even builds fictional universes which he calls oddly enough *Anatomy of Criticism*. Frye wants his system to "reforge the broken links between creation and knowledge, art and science, myth and concept"; [11] but actually his criticism is an elaborate fiction which loses all relation to knowledge, science, and concept. All manner of substitutions, condensations, and identifications are allowed in this dream universe. As Frye admits: "The literary universe is a universe in which everything is potentially identical with everything else." [12] Criticism, like literature and like mythology, becomes, in his own words, "largely an art of misleading analogies and mistaken identities." [13] A fanciful structure is erected which has as much contact with actual literary history as Blake's *Jerusalem* or Yeats's *A Vision* has with recorded history. It can hardly

9. *Intentions* (New York, 1894) , pp. 200–202.
10. *La Vie littéraire* (Paris, 1888) , Preface, Vol. I.
11. *Anatomy of Criticism* (Princeton, N.J., 1956) , p. 354.
12. *Ibid.*, p. 124.
13. *Fables of Identity: Studies in Poetic Mythology* (New York, 1963) , p. 35.

surprise us that the weird, whimsical, and utterly fantastic interpretations of Greek myths propounded by Ruskin later in his life in *The
Cestus of Aglaia* (1865) and *The Queen of the Air* (1869) have been
hailed as forerunners of Frye's and Yeats's archetypal criticism.[14] One
might recognize the ingenuity and imaginative inventiveness of these
writers and might come to think of this criticism as a new literary
genre. But it must be distinguished from criticism, which upholds
ideals of correctness of interpretation, observes the laws of evidence,
and must aim, ultimately, at a body of knowledge which we hesitate to
call "science" only because the natural scientists have pre-empted the
term in English.

The invasion and even subjugation of criticism by poetic or purely
imaginative methods, whether in the style of Pater or of Northrop
Frye, has not furthered the cause of criticism. The opposite imperial-
ism, the invasion of poetry by criticism, also has damaging effects for
poetry. We hear much of the share of criticism in the actual process of
poetic composition. Eliot, for instance, said that "the labour of sifting,
combining, constructing, expunging, correcting, testing," is "a fright-
ful toil as much critical as creative. I maintain even that the criticism
employed by a trained and skilled writer on his own work is the most
vital, the highest kind of criticism." [15] But one wonders whether this
self-criticism is criticism in the usual sense or merely a metaphor for
the labor of composing. The poet, Croce remarks in this context,
"cannot complete his work without self-government, without an inner
check, without accepting and rejecting, without trial and error." But
calling this criticism is like using the term "obstetric criticism" for
"the spasms and pauses and new starts of a woman in the labor of
childbirth." [16] We need not go so far as Croce in denying even a
similarity between the process of composition and criticism proper to
see that we are dealing here with a separate problem: the share of
intellect in the creative process. It has been debated endlessly, in older
times as a conflict between inspiration and craft, and more recently as
a conflict between the subconscious and technical manipulation. Coleridge's fib about writing "Kubla Khan" after awaking from a profound
sleep in a trance interrupted by the "person on business from Por-
lock" [17] contrasts with Poe's stunt or hoax in "The Philosophy of
Composition," of describing how the work on "The Raven" pro-

14. Ed. Harold Bloom, *The Literary Criticism of John Ruskin* (Garden City,
N. Y., 1965), Introduction, p. xvi.

15. "The Function of Criticism," *Selected Essays* (London, 1932), p. 30.

16. *La Poesia* (4th ed.; Bari, 1946), pp. 13–14.

17. For a full discussion, see Elisabeth Schneider, *Coleridge, Opium and Kubla
Khan* (Chicago, 1953), esp. pp. 22 ff.

ceeded, "step by step, to its completion with the precision and rigid consequence of a mathematical problem."[18]

But these conflicting accounts of the poets have not, to my mind, contributed much either to an elucidation of the poetic process or even to a psychology of writing. T. S. Eliot thought that "the penetration of the poetic by the introspective critical activity is carried to the limit" by Valéry in several essays.[19] But Valéry actually cannot say more than that a poem might arise from the most diverse stimuli: "an empty piece of paper; a little free time; a slip of the tongue; a misreading; a pen which fits the hand agreeably."[20] He tells us only about empirical occasions, suggestions, and sequences. We can observe the same thing in ourselves even as we write private letters or learned papers: they start somewhere, somehow. A Censor (as Auden calls him with a better term than critic)[21] is at work in us as in the poet. Surprisingly, most modern poets support the inspiration version of the poetic process, although they might not like the term. For what else is being described even by the highly rational Valéry when he tells us that "the poetic start is perfectly irregular, inconstant, involuntary, and fragile. . . . We lose it just as we find it by accident"?[22] I need only allude to Rilke's description of the ecstasy in which he composed the *Duino Elegies* or to Yeats's well-known lines:

> God guard me from those thoughts men think
> In the mind alone,
> He that sings a lasting song
> Thinks in a marrow bone.[23]

The poet, it seems to me, has told us little about the creative process, whether he is Valéry (M. Teste, that is, "Head") or the surrealist relying on his subconscious and on automatic writing. The poet has not learned much or taught us much about the poetic process. We owe more to scholars who have studied sources, like John Livingston Lowes in *The Road to Xanadu,* or to the students of drafts and revisions, if they are more than just textual critics, and even to the psychologists

18. See comment in my *History of Modern Criticism,* III, 159 ff., and the opinion of Baudelaire quoted on p. 323.

19. *To Criticize the Critic* (London, 1965), p. 41.

20. *L'Invention* (Paris, 1938), p. 150. A different translation in *Aesthetics,* trans. Ralph Manheim (New York, 1964), p. 69.

21. *The Dyer's Hand,* p. 33.

22. *Variété* (Paris, 1945), V, 138; also in *The Art of Poetry,* trans. Denis Folliot (New York, 1956), p. 60.

23. "A Prayer for Old Age," *Variorum Edition of the Poems of W. B. Yeats,* ed. P. Allt and R. K. Alspach (New York, 1957), p. 553.

and psychoanalysts, or to such amateur philosophers as Arthur Koestler.[24]

But the oldest incursion of criticism into poetry, or, if you prefer, the oldest alliance between criticism and poetry, is versified criticism: Horace's "De Arte poetica," and, since the Renaissance, Vida's "Poetica," Boileau's "Art poétique," and, of course, Pope's "Essay on Criticism." The genre which is simply a version of the didactic genre of versified philosophy, astronomy, or history seems to have died out in the eighteenth century, possibly with Akenside's "The Pleasures of the Imagination," but actually it reappears, in new forms, even in the twentieth century. Verlaine's anti-rhetorical pamphlet, *L'Art poétique*, is in rhyme, and rather recently Karl Shapiro has written an unrhymed *Essay on Rime*. In general, one can dismiss these poems, if we judge them as poetry, but one should recognize that some of them, particularly Pope's "Essay on Criticism," display some aesthetic qualities: design, metrical skill, and verbal wit. With the increasing understanding of the nature of poetry, such rhymed or blank verse expositions of abstract ideas have come to be felt as unpoetic and have fallen into desuetude. Still, some poets have tried in their poetry to speak of poetry and the poet: to create something which has been called "meta-poetry" as we speak of "meta-language." This "meta-poetry" is largely concerned with the self-definition of the poet and with his mission or function. It must be associated with the modern questioning of his status as a seer, priest, or sage. In Germany particularly, Hölderlin reasserted in poetry the sacred mission of the poet, and more recently Rilke has in "The Seventh Duino Elegy" asked the poet to transform the whole visible world into an "inner space." In France, Mallarmé composed his "Toast funèbre" for Théophile Gautier, in which the eternalizing function of art "by a solemn agitation in the air of words" is asserted with desperate defiance. In recent American poetry I might refer to Wallace Stevens' "Notes toward A Supreme Fiction" or to "The Idea of Order at Key West," which addresses a French critic, Ramon Fernandez, to praise the "blessed rage for order, . . . the maker's rage to order words." Or we might think of Archibald Mac-Leish's "Ars Poetica" with its often misunderstood concluding lines:

A poem should not mean
But be.

We might even think of meta-poetry as the evocation of other poets in verse: Ben Jonson's eulogy of Shakespeare or Arnold's sonnet on

24. Arthur Koestler, *The Act of Creation* (London, 1964).

98

Shakespeare might qualify; or Swinburne's premature elegy on Baudelaire; or even Shelley's *Adonais;* or, in the second part of *Faust,* Goethe's Euphorion, who is meant to represent Byron.[25] In the wide sense of poetry about poets and poetry, meta-poetry would have to include Virgil in the *Divine Comedy* and Goethe's play on Torquato Tasso and all the many dramas and poems about artists in its wake. The ramifications of such a topic are endless, its limitations hard to define. The poet has, throughout history, built up his image, described his mission, put forward his claims, defended his activity, and spoken well or ill of his fellow poets—in verse, as a poet, and inevitably also in prose, as a critic or simply as a man who as any other man has literary opinions.

In the last decades in England and the United States the apology for poetry by poets has assumed new forms: it has become a counterattack against criticism, science, and the intellect in general, a campaign which is, of course, waged with the weapons of the intellect and in works of criticism. Some of it is simply anti-criticism, anti-intellectualism, like Karl Shapiro's onslaught in his collection of essays, *In Defense of Ignorance.* Shapiro repeats the old argument that "criticism flourishes when literature has failed," but he does not recognize that criticism really flourishes today. If it does it is the kind of criticism he detests. He simply shies away from "criticism as a branch of philosophy." "The poet and the poet-in-us-all have no business hanging around philosophy." He recommends as the only genuine criticism, "creative criticism," a "work of art about another work of art," but he continues to write criticism of a type which could not possibly claim to be artistic, while saying, "poet and critic must draw apart, and beyond this I have no message." [26] Similarly, the late Randall Jarrell in an article, "The Age of Criticism," voices the understandable dismay of a poet at the sheer proliferation of criticism in our time. But the remedy he proposes is merely the old personal, impressionist criticism. " 'Principles' or 'standards' of excellence are either specifically harmful or generally useless; the critic has nothing to go by except his experience as a human being and a reader, and is the personification of empiricism." Criticism is seen as strictly subordinated to works of art. "Critics exist simply to help us with works of art." Criticism exists merely "for the sake of the plays and stories and poems it criticizes." Jarrell seems not to be aware of the possibility of theory or history which might not

25. See the interesting collection, *Poems on Poetry: The Mirror's Garland,* ed. Robert Wallace and James G. Taaffe (New York, 1965).
26. *In Defense of Ignorance* (New York, 1965), pp. 6, 18, 31–32.

be dependent on the enhancement of the reader's enjoyment. He uses the oldest and most unconvincing argument that the poet alone knows what poetry is. He ridicules some critics discussing Wordsworth: *"they knew how poems and novels are put together, and Wordsworth . . . did not, but had just put them together.* In the same way, if a pig wandered up to you during a bacon-judging contest, you would say impatiently, 'Go away, pig! What do you know about bacon?' " [27] But this is literally true of the pig. It does not know anything about bacon, its flavor or price, and could not appraise bacon in so many words. When a famous poet was proposed for a professorship at Harvard, his appointment was rejected when a witty opponent argued that one would not make an elephant Professor of Zoology.

Shapiro and Jarrell belong to a venerable tradition: that of empiricism, particularly Anglo-Saxon empiricism, suspicious of all theory. John Stuart Mill, in 1831, in his *Spirit of the Age* complained of this aversion. "He is a *theorist:* and the word which expresses the highest and noblest effort of human intelligence is turned into a byword of derision." [28] Such a position amounts to a retreat or the wish for a retreat into a world untouched by science, the intellect, and reason. It is obscurantist in its consequences.

The poet's attack on criticism is more formidable when it comes from convictions inherent in a different philosophy. The most interesting case is that of T. S. Eliot. I alluded to his lecture, "To Criticize the Critic," which indulges in an almost embarrassing self-depreciation. "Humility" was its last word, and it was the last word I ever heard him pronounce. But this self-disparagement is not a chance event in Eliot's intellectual biography. It grows out of his concept of criticism, held since his youth, and was prepared for by similar statements. In the Minnesota lecture, "The Frontiers of Criticism" (1956) —which was, I hear, attended by five thousand persons—Eliot paid no attention to new trends in criticism, but commented on the criticism of sources exemplified in Lowes's *The Road to Xanadu* (1926) and on biographical criticism of Wordsworth by Herbert Read and F. W. Bateson, concluding, rightly I think, that neither source-study nor biography can define the nature of poetry. "When the poem has been made, something new has happened, something that cannot be wholly explained by *anything that went before.*" But then Eliot turns against what in this country is called "explication" or "close reading"; he criticizes a book, *Interpretations,* edited by John Wain, which contains twelve essays by English critics, each analyzing a well-known poem,

27. *Poetry and the Age* (New York, 1955) , pp. 81, 84, 65, 66–67.
28. Ed. Frederick von Hayek (Chicago, 1942) , p. 21.

from Shakespeare's "The Phoenix and the Turtle" to Yeats's "Among School Children." Eliot describes the method: take a poem "without reference to the author or to his other work, analyse it stanza by stanza and line by line, and extract, squeeze, tease, press every drop of meaning out of it that one can. It might be called the lemon-squeezer school of criticism." Eliot complains mildly that this is "a very tiring way of passing the time" and that in reading the interpretation of his own "The Love Song of J. Alfred Prufrock" he had "one or two minor surprises." But he also makes the more serious general objection that the analyses damaged the appreciation of these familiar poems. "I found I was slow to recover my previous feeling about the poems. It was as if someone had taken a machine to pieces and left one with the task of reassembling the parts." The argument is the old one: analysis spoils enjoyment, and criticism must serve enjoyment. Eliot warns of "the danger of pursuing criticism as if it was a science" and professes not to recall even "a single book or essay, or the name of a single critic, as representative of the kind of impressionistic criticism which aroused my ire thirty-three years ago." [29] (Thirty-three years because Eliot is referring to the essay, "The Function of Criticism," which dates from 1923.) But he might have looked into *The Sacred Wood* (1920) and found there expressions of his ire against Swinburne, John Addington Symonds, and Arthur Symons. In effect, Eliot in these last lectures has become another defender of appreciation and has abandoned his older ambition for criticism generally and his own criticism as "the common pursuit of true judgment." [30]

The later surrender to subjectivism and appreciation is, however, clearly prepared for in his early unsatisfactory theory of criticism. Eliot dismissed interpretation as a necessary evil, a makeshift for our imperfections as readers. "If we lived [a work] completely we should need no interpretation" is Eliot's singularly unhelpful conclusion in recommending G. Wilson Knight's *The Wheel of Fire*.[31] It is like saying "If I were God, I would need no theology." While interpretation is tolerated as a necessary evil, judgment is surprisingly forbidden to the critic. "The critic must not coerce, and must not make judgments of worse and better." Judgment arises somehow from "elucidation," which seems to differ from interpretation, although I am not sure in what way it could. "The critic," Eliot declares, "must simply elucidate: the reader will form the correct judgment for himself." [32] But it is hard

29. *On Poetry and Poets*, pp. 103, 112, 113, 114, 117.
30. "The Function of Criticism," *Selected Essays*, p. 25.
31. *The Wheel of Fire* (London, 1930), Introduction, p. xix.
32. "The Perfect Critic," *The Sacred Wood*, p. 10.

to believe that the early Eliot could have meant the rejection of both interpretation and judgment literally; he wanted rather to protest against arbitrary interpretations and against dogmatic rankings of authors. Actually, he constantly recommended interpreters, such as G. Wilson Knight, S. L. Bethell, and even the dreary Leone Vivante. He himself made judgments about "better and worse" in almost every sentence of his criticism. Ranking, judging, is the secret of his success as a critic. One wanted to hear that Crashaw "was a finished master, and Keats and Shelley were apprentices with immense possibilities before them," [33] that Campion was a greater poet than Herrick, or Dryden than Pope.

But in theory, Eliot even then upheld the view that there is no objective meaning to a work of art. "A poem may appear to mean very different things to different readers, and all these meanings may be different from what the author thought he meant," seems a reasonable observation from which Eliot draws the conclusion that "the reader's interpretation may differ from the author's and be equally valid—it may even be better. There may be much more in a poem than the author was aware of." [34] This is still acceptable as a defense of the accrual of meaning which occurs in the course of history: *Hamlet* cannot be reduced to the interpretation which Shakespeare might have given to it. But Eliot is on dangerous ground when, in a conversation reported by Nevill Coghill, he denied that there is a correct interpretation of his *Sweeney Agonistes*. When he saw a production in Oxford, he was "astonished" by it, and felt that it ran completely counter to his own interpretation. To the question, "But if the two meanings are contradictory, is not one right and the other wrong? Must not the author be right?" Eliot answered, "Not necessarily, do you think? Why is either wrong?" [35] Eliot, like Valéry who spoke of "creative misunderstanding" and went so far as to say that there is "no true meaning to a text," does not see that the divorce between work and reader cannot be complete and that there remains the problem of the "correctness" of interpretation. We may debate the theories of Coleridge, Bradley, Stoll, Ernest Jones, and even Eliot about *Hamlet,* but we must reject the view propounded in a full-length book that Hamlet was a woman in disguise in love with Horatio. "The meaning is what the poem means to different sensitive readers" [36] is Eliot's conclusion,

---

33. *For Lancelot Andrewes* (London, 1928), p. 120.
34. "The Music of Poetry," *On Poetry and Poets,* p. 30.
35. *T. S. Eliot: A Symposium,* ed. R. March and Tambimutti (London, 1948), p. 86.
36. "The Frontiers of Criticism," *On Poetry and Poets,* p. 113.

which is saved from mere anarchical relativism only by the question-begging adjective "sensitive." The whole theory of criticism propounded by Eliot is in total contradiction to his objectivistic philosophy which aims at a definition of the tradition and must assume its truth. As I have argued before,[37] Eliot's criticism suffers from the conflict between his emotionalist concept of poetry, his denial that poetry is knowledge or even any kind of knowledge, and the dogmatic ideological superstructure of classicism and later of orthodoxy. With the growing emphasis on appreciation and enjoyment and the growing distaste for analysis, "close reading," or what he considered science, Eliot has widened the gulf between the two sides of his critical practice, his sensibility and his orthodoxy, and has committed himself to a double standard in criticism: appreciation and "supervision of the tradition by orthodoxy" [38] which again dissolves the unity of the work of art. Eliot has abandoned aesthetic criticism to the appreciators, to the subjective relativists, in order to uphold what in practice is didactic, ideological criticism ruled by his idea of right religion.

The two eminent American poets who are also eminent literary critics, John Crowe Ransom and Allen Tate, did not turn against criticism as Eliot did, but they were pushed by their theories into views of literary criticism which deny intellectual coherence and historical growth to the enterprise. Ransom—contrary to a common view which considers him peculiarly provincial and "native"—had been a student of philosophy at Oxford. His poetic theories obviously developed from his study of Bergson, Collingwood, and the English expounder of Bergson, T. E. Hulme. Ransom's criticism of abstraction, his distinction between logical structure and irrelevant texture in a poem, his attack on the poetry of ideas, and his advocacy of a poetry of things fit into the whole Bergsonian irrationalistic trend of the time. Imagism, Rilke and his *Dinggedicht,* and Francis Ponge had similar aims. Ransom holds a view of history as a continuous widening of the dualism between science and art by reason of the aggressions of science. "As science more and more completely reduces the world to its types and forms, art, replying, must invest it again with body." [39] Ransom, with his article, "Criticism, Inc.," and his book *The New Criticism,* did much to define the movement named by him and to give it academic status. But in his theory of criticism, expounded in the chapter, "Wanted: An Ontological Critic," he limits the vocation of criticism drastically to distinguishing between the range of words as meaning

37. See "The Criticism of T. S. Eliot," *Sewanee Review,* LXIV (1956), 398–443.
38. *After Strange Gods* (New York, 1934), p. 67.
39. *The World's Body* (New York, 1938), p. 198.

and the range of words as sound, and especially between determinate and indeterminate meaning. Since "the indeterminate thing creeps in by the back door of metrical necessity," [40] much of what Ransom considers criticism par excellence is a study of meter, or of the relation between sound and meaning, or a study of metaphors and diction. Ransom, in his later writings, experimented restlessly with his terminology: the dualism of structure and texture appears under new guises as the contrast between the Freudian ego and id. Or he replaces the pair, structure and texture, by a triad of metaphor, logic, and meter; or he adopts the term "icon" for "image" from Charles Morris, or the "Concrete Universal" from Hegel via Wimsatt. Poetry, however, remains always concrete and he thus rejects as extra-poetic the Chicago Aristotelians' concern for plot, or that of Yvor Winters for morality. But ultimately Ransom embraces a version of the "imitation" theory himself. The little world of objects "sets up a small version of our natural world in its original dignity, not the laborious world of affairs. Indeed, the little world is the imitation of our ancient Paradise, when we inhabited it in innocence." [41] Criticism thus becomes "substantial," referential, and a double standard is introduced or at least permitted: aesthetic and ideological criticism. Ransom defends "the rights of the intellectuals (the moralists or religionists) to isolate the ideas and discuss them on their intellectual merits; inasmuch as the ideas are surely in the poetry." "This is a poetry that can be taken apart. And yet if it is really a poetry it cannot be hurt; and Kantians [and here Ransom seems to proclaim himself a Kantian] can come back to the whole poetry and see what is poetical about it." The dualistic theory of poetry, with its logical structure and indeterminate, contingent texture, has taken its toll. Ransom leaves criticism with two themes— both outside of art: "natural beauty" and "morals." No wonder that in an article on Cleanth Brooks called "Why critics don't go mad?" he speaks of the critic's "bad sense of lostness." [42]

Allen Tate's views of criticism have changed considerably in his development. He used to be extremely effective in his attacks on academic literary scholarship. The lecture, "Miss Emily and the Bibliographer" (1940), made a fervent plea for the moral obligation of judging, and made trenchant criticisms of the academic teaching of literature. Like Ransom, Tate was driven by his disapproval of science —which in him can be called contempt and even hatred—into an anti-intellectualistic position which affected also his theory of criticism. He

40. *The New Criticism* (Norfolk, Conn., 1941), pp. 301, 303.
41. *Poems and Essays* (New York, 1955), p. 100.
42. *Ibid.*, pp. 185, 147.

differs, however, from Ransom not only in tone—his is passionate and sometimes turgid, while Ransom's is urbane and often whimsical—but in philosophical allegiance. Although Ransom wrote his first book, *God Without Thunder,* in defense of a fundamentalist religion, and although he shared the Southern Agrarianism of his Nashville friends and pupils, his view of poetry always remained secular and even basically hedonistic. Poetry is a celebration of the world and of the poet's love of the world, which is being spoiled by the ugly industrial civilization of the North, and by Science robbing it of its enchantment and dense particularity. Tate, even very early, is much more concerned with a historical view of the decay of our civilization through science and liberalism, seen as a disintegration of man and his support, religion. Poetry, with Tate, particularly after his conversion to Roman Catholicism, becomes an analogue of religion, a human paradigm of the Word, a parallel to the Incarnation. The role of criticism dwindles, or rather the critic becomes absorbed in the guardian of revealed truth. However, there is an apocalyptic, priestly tone to the speech, "The Man of Letters in the Modern World," which rejects the task of communication between men for that of a true communion through love assigned to the "man of letters," while the critic is reduced to the job of "preserving the integrity, the purity, and the reality of language" against the corruptions of the mass media.[43] While the poet and the man of letters are still given exalted functions as masters of the symbolic imagination and re-creators of the image of man, critics and criticism are relegated to a nook and cranny of the intellectual universe. For himself, Tate, like Eliot, disavows system and describes himself as a "casual essayist of whom little consistency can be expected," writing from "a mere point of view," which, however, must not be called relative.[44]

In a late essay, "Is Literary Criticism Possible?" Tate denies that we will ever know this, and discusses first the question of teaching criticism in a university. He hands literary history and sociology to the social sciences and leaves criticism in the university with only one task: the rhetorical study of language. He decides that one cannot teach students to "evaluate" works of literature though this may be "not less absurd than to try to evaluate them oneself." Even the other possible task of criticism, the communication of insights, is declared to be impossible of being taught to others. Insights "can be only exhibited" is Tate's odd conclusion, though it is difficult to see why the "exhibi-

---

43. *The Man of Letters in the Modern World: Selected Essays: 1928–1955* (New York, 1955) , p. 20.
44. *Ibid.,* Preface, pp. 6–7.

tion" of insights does not communicate them and thus teach them to the right students. In the second part of the paper, Tate ignores the quite separate question of pedagogy in an American university and confronts the aims of literary criticism in the abstract. In a scrappy and dense list of problems he says mainly negative things about criticism. Criticism is always inferior to creation. "It is always *about* something else." It is thus parasitic and "perpetually obsolescent and replaceable"—a view which can be upheld only if we confine ourselves to day-by-day reviewers, to the necessary middlemen between author and audience, but which is obviously false if we think of theory, poetics, and history. Tate, of course, recognizes that there is the more systematic and methodical, the purer, criticism which "tends more and more to *sound* like philosophical discourse." He distinguishes three methods: aesthetics, which he dismisses curtly, as "from its point of view it is difficult to say anything about literature that is not merely pretentious." Then Tate allows "stylistics," within its narrow limits, and historical reconstruction, which is not criticism proper. In a next congested paragraph, Tate objects to philosophical criticism: criticism which appeals to a philosophical authority in which the critic does not believe. No evidence is presented for why the critic could not believe in a philosopher and use him. We are simply warned, "The language of criticism had better not, then, try to be univocal." There is, how-ever, one type of criticism which finds favor in Tate's eyes though he asks only tentatively: "What is the primary office of criticism? Is it to expound and to elucidate, with as little distortion as possible, the knowledge of life contained by the novel or the poem or the play? What critic has ever done this?" One would think that all moral and social critics were doing nothing else for centuries, but possibly Tate means something very different from what is usually called knowledge of life. Finally he asks, "Is literary criticism possible without a crite-rion of absolute truth? Would a criterion of absolute truth make literary criticism as we know it unnecessary?" Knowing Tate's con-victions from other texts, an affirmative answer is required. In the light of the truth of Revelation, criticism is unnecessary, although immediately afterward Tate declares it "perpetually necessary and, in the very nature of its middle position between imagination and philos-ophy, perpetually impossible." [45] At risk of being called a ration-alist, I consider such exalted eloquence a surrender to unreason, an evasion of the task in front of us. The man of faith has destroyed the critic in Tate.

45. *Ibid.,* pp. 162–74.

I have demonstrated the anti-criticism of five recent poet-critics at some length in order to show that the union of poet and critic is not always a happy one. No doubt, the poet-critic will not only stay with us but will multiply as a type, since the poet can no longer be a seer, a magician, a popular philosopher and moralist, and even a popular entertainer without self-consciousness. But the union of poet and critic is not necessarily good for either poetry or criticism. It seems to me an illusion that it restores the original whole man, the *uomo universale* of the Renaissance. Our time is obsessed by the fear of "alienation," which is often ascribed to specialization and, in Marx (but not in Hegel), serves as a criticism of the modern division of labor. But the Marxist solution which would abolish the artist's profession in the classless Utopia where, says Marx, there "will not be any painters, but at the most men, who among other things, also paint" [46] is an absurdly idyllic dream. It would give us Churchills and Eisenhowers exercising their Sunday hobby, while the whole history of painting demonstrates the success of the full-time professional and specialist: Titian, Rembrandt, Velasquez, Rubens, and Cézanne. The same is true of poetry: the great poet is absorbed and even possessed by his task. It is a mistake to glorify his distractions or to minimize the obstacles in his way. There were a few shining examples of great poet-critics in history —Dante, Goethe, Coleridge come most readily to mind—but I am not sure that it is right to describe them as successful cases of a union of the two; rather they managed somehow to alternate poetry and criticism. Dante wrote *De Vulgari Eloquentia* and then the *Divine Comedy;* Goethe, *Faust,* and in between the two parts, the treatise on "Simple Imitation, Manner and Style"; Coleridge, "The Rime of the Ancient Mariner," and years later, *Biographia Literaria.* They were not torn by inner conflicts between instinct and intellect, but rather were poets at one moment and critics at another. Our time has reacted sharply against the "pure" art, the "pure" scholarship, and the "pure" criticism of the early twentieth century. We don't want to be specialists; we want to be whole men; we want to reconcile the conscious and the unconscious, the life of the senses and the intellect. We want to have poet-critics. We can hope for them, but as the Devil's advocate I can recommend beatification only in very rare cases, with veritable saints who have accomplished the miracle of reconciliation.

46. Karl Marx and Friedrich Engels, *Über Kunst und Literatur,* ed. Michael Lipschitz (Berlin, 1948), p. 90.

Index

WHERE NUMEROUS ENTRIES occur for a single author, general references are followed by the author's works, listed alphabetically in the following order of genres: collected poetry, individual poems, fiction, drama, essays or criticism, letters, selected and collected works, and critical commentaries on the author. Entries in parentheses following an italicized book title are to be regarded as items to be found in that work.

INDEX

Ravel, Maurice: "Bolero," 83
Raysor, T. M.: ed. *Coleridge's Miscellaneous Criticism,* 33n
Read, Herbert, 100
Rembrandt (van Rijn), 107
Richards, I. A., 30, 49; *Coleridge on Imagination,*" 27, 30, 41n; *Principles of Literary Criticism,* 49
Rilke, Rainer Maria, x, xi, xii, 60–80 *passim,* 97, 98, 103; *Book of Pictures,* 72, 73; *Duino Elegies,* 77, 78, 78n, 97; "The Second Duino Elegy," 77, 78; "The Seventh Duino Elegy," 98; *New Poems,* 62, 74, 77; *Sonnets to Orpheus,* 75; "Early Apollo," 73; "Death of the Poet," 76; "Hetärengräber," 77; Orpheus, Eurydice, Hermes," 73; "The Unicorn," 62, 63; *Sämtliche Werke,* 62n, 72n, 74n, 75n, 76n, 78n
Rodin, François Auguste René, 79
Roethke, Theodore, 90
Ross, Robert, 52
Rubens, Peter Paul, 203
Ruskin, John, 46, 96; *The Cestus of Aglaia,* 96; *The Queen of the Air,* 96
Ruth (Bible), 19
Rylands Library (Manchester), 30

Sainte-Beuve, Charles-Augustin, 93
Santayana, George, 70
Schiller, Johann Christoph Friedrich von, 94
Schneider, Elisabeth: *Coleridge, Opium and Kubla Khan,* 96n
Sewell, Elizabeth, vii, ix, 73; *The Orphic Voice,* 73n
Shakespeare, William, 10, 27, 36, 52, 53, 89, 95, 99, 101, 102; *Sonnets,* 52; "The Phoenix and the Turtle," 9n, 10, 101; *Hamlet,* 22, 53, 102; *King Henry IV, Part I,* 45; *King Lear,* 22
Shapiro, Karl, xiii, 99, 100; *Essay on Rime,* 98; *In Defense of Ignorance,* 99, 99n
Shaw, Priscilla Washburn: *Rilke, Valéry and Yeats: The Domain of the Self,* 71, 76, 76n
Shelley, Percy Bysshe, 36, 84, 102; "Adonais," 99; "To a Skylark," 20, 24
Simonides (of Ceos), 4
Snodgrass, W. D., 83
Snyder, Alice D., 30, 34, 35; *Coleridge on Logic and Learning,* 30, 34n, 35, 43n
Sontag, Susan, 54
Sophocles, *Oedipus Rex,* 22

Spender, Stephen: trans. Rilke's *Duino Elegies* with J. B. Leishman, 78, 78n
Spitzer, Leo, 8, 8n; "The 'Ode on a Grecian Urn,' or Content vs. Metagrammar," 8n; *Essays on English and American Literature,* ed. Anna Hatcher, 8n
Stein, Gertrude, 83
Stendhal (Henri Beyle), 45
Stevens, Wallace, x, xi, xii, 25, 60–80 *passim,* 98; *Harmonium,* 61; *Collected Poems,* 63n, 67n, 68n, 69n, 70n; ("Anecdote of the Jar," 24, 25, 25n; "The Comedian as the Letter C," 67; "The Glass of Water," 68; "The Idea of Order at Key West," 98; "Landscape with Boat," 68; "The Man with the Blue Guitar," 68; "Le Monocle de mon Oncle," 67; Notes toward a Supreme Fiction," 69, 98; "Nude Starting on a Spring Voyage," 68; "An Ordinary Evening in New Haven," 70; "Peter Quince at the Clavier," 66, 67; "The Pure Good of Theory," 68; "The Snow Man," 68; "Sunday Morning," 66, 67; "Woman Looking at a Vase of Flowers," 63, 65); *A Necessary Angel:* ("Imagination and Value," 65, 65n, 66, 66n, 69, 69n; "The Noble Rider and the Sound of Words," 65); *Opus Posthumous:* ("A Collect of Philosophy," 60)
Stoll, Elmer E., 102
Swinburne, Algernon Charles, 95, 101; "Ave atque Vale," 99
Symbolist movement, 62, 64, 76, 77, 79
Symonds, John Addington, 99
Symons, Arthur, 47, 99

Taaffe, James G. *See* Robert Wallace
Taine, Hippolyte, 53
Tambimutti: *T. S. Eliot: a Symposium,* ed. with R. March, 102n
Tate, Allen, xiii, 103, 104–6; "Miss Emily and the Bibliographer," 104; *The Man of Letters in the Modern World: Selected Essays: 1928–1955:* ("The Man of Letters in the Modern World," 105; "Is Literary Criticism Possible?" 105, 106)
Thomas, Dylan, 88
Titian (Tiziano Vecellio), 107
Trinity College (Dublin), 45

Valéry, Paul, 97, 102; *L'Invention,* 97, 97n; *Aesthetics,* trans. Ralph Man-

COLOPHON

THE TEXT OF THIS BOOK is set in ten-point Baskerville, two points leaded. This handsome, truly "English" type face was designed about 1760 by John Baskerville, the most notable type founder and printer of his day. Born in 1706, Baskerville was trained as a writing-master, and the type face for which he is known reflects his proficiency in that art. In general, this face forms a transition between the "old style" designs of William Caslon, after which most of Baskerville's letters are modeled, and the rather severely regular formality of the "modern" designs of Giambattista Bodoni. The display types are Goudy Old Style, designed by the great twentieth-century American typographer Frederic Goudy. The paper for the book was manufactured by the S. D. Warren Company, and the binding cloths by Columbia Mills, Inc. Composition, printing, and binding were done by Kingsport Press, Inc. The typography, binding design, and jacket are by Paul Randall Mize.